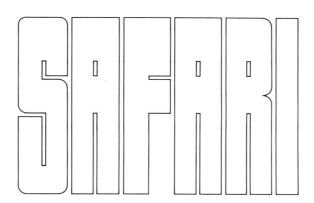

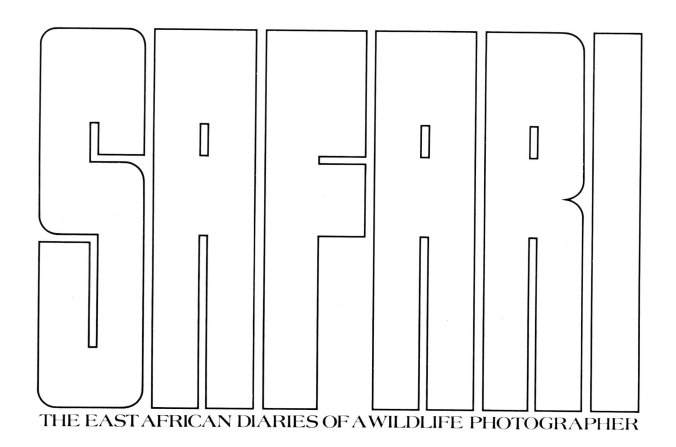

SAFARI

THE EAST AFRICAN DIARIES OF A WILDLIFE PHOTOGRAPHER

Photographs by Günter Ziesler
Diary notes by Angelika Hofer

Consulting editor Nigel Sitwell

COLT ASSOCIATES

This book was produced in association with
Bruce Coleman Limited

Published by Colt Associates
The Old School
Brewhouse Hill
Wheathampstead
Hertfordshire AL4 8AN

ISBN 0 951 15580 6

AN EDDISON · SADD EDITION

Edited, designed and produced by
Eddison/Sadd Editions Limited
2 Kendall Place, London W1H 3AH

Phototypeset by Bookworm Typesetting,
Manchester, England
Origination by Columbia Offset, Singapore
Printed and bound by Tonsa,
San Sebastian, Spain

CONTENTS

ACKNOWLEDGMENTS

We should like to thank:

Pritpal and Simrin Singh Sohanpaul, who made
their home in Nairobi our 'African home' and helped
us in every possible way.

Tim Samuels and Murray Levet from Governor's
Camp, for untold kindness and generosity.

Bruce Coleman, whose enthusiasm
and encouragement made it possible to create
this book.

Nigel Sitwell for his work on the diaries.

Ian Jackson and Nigel Partridge of Eddison/Sadd
Editions for the cooperation they offered us during
the selection of photographs and planning the
layout of the book.

The government and the people of Kenya for their
determination to preserve their wildlife heritage for
future generations to enjoy.

Günter Ziesler
and Angelika Hofer

INTRODUCTION
BY NIGEL SITWELL

Hundreds of thousands, probably millions, of people have visited the famous safarilands of eastern and southern Africa during the last two or three decades, and it is certain that the vast majority have carried cameras. The number of photographs of African wildlife that have been taken must, therefore, be enormous. And yet, while obviously very profitable for the photographic trade, it is fair to assume that only a small proportion of this tidal wave of images is above average in quality.

The fact is that taking a good photograph of an animal, as of anything else, is not easy. It may not be hard to produce an adequate picture, but an excellent one requires technical ability, visual flair, patience, a knowledge of animal behaviour, and a host of other skills. Luck is an important ingredient, but good luck tends to come to those who already have what it takes in other ways.

What kind of person makes a great wildlife photographer? I have met quite a few, and they are as varied as any cross-section of humanity you may care to choose – short, tall, male, female, extrovert, introvert, highly qualified, or self-taught. But they do share certain attributes. A love of wild places, a passionate interest in animals, unlimited patience, and, of course, technical competence, though this is usually built up through experience.

Günter Ziesler, who took the remarkable pictures in this book, is undoubtedly one of the world's best photographers of wildlife, though his background contains no clue as to the calling he would eventually follow.

He was born in Munich in 1939. Nobody in his family ever showed the slightest concern for natural history. 'I can find no interest of this sort, going back to my grandfather and grandmother. Some of my family were farmers, but they don't seem to have been interested *in* nature, so much as earning a living *from* it. Nor has my family ever shown any scientific or artistic talents. It is strange. I don't know where my own interest in nature came from…It just came.'

And it developed very early, it seems, for Günter can remember going to his grandfather's farm when he was about three or four years old and being intrigued by an album of cigarette cards. These showed pictures of the German colonies, such as German East Africa, and he recalls especially those of Mount Kilimanjaro and African wildlife. 'I was fascinated by pictures of any kind as a very small child,' says Günter, 'and I still am. When I was older I started going to the movies, and spent hours and hours in the cinema in my twenties. That was when I had more spare time, before I started taking photographs myself.'

His interest in animals also began early, for in his childhood he kept frogs and newts, snakes and lizards, in glass vivaria that he built himself. Günter believes that his preoccupation with nature and wildlife would have led inevitably to some appropriate career involving these interests. He remembers that his first ambition was to become a forest ranger, or perhaps a zoologist. It was some years, however, before he was able to realize any such ambitions.

Günter's father worked as a delivery driver for a chain of large stores, which was very hard work in those days, with much lifting and carrying. He wanted his son to have an easier life than he had had, and the best thing he could think of was to be able to sit in an office. So the young Günter was encouraged in this direction, and in due course went to work for Unilever.

Nevertheless, life was not all sitting in an office and going to the cinema, for in 1958 Günter started taking photographs as a hobby. His first camera was an old Voigtlander, which he used mainly to photograph animals in zoos, but wild animals also. However, as he points out, this camera had an unsophisticated focusing mechanism, and it was hard to take good pictures with it. The results were certainly not very encouraging.

But he persisted, gradually progressing through better and better cameras, and his results began to improve. In 1970 Günter went on his first long trip, to Turkey for a holiday, during which he visited Lake Manyas, a magnificent sanctuary for water birds to the south of the Sea of Marmara. 'This holiday', says Günter, 'proved to be a turning point. For the first time I took what I considered to be some really good photographs, and I also met Udo Hirsch, a professional wildlife photographer from Cologne.'

Günter returned to Lake Manyas the following year, and again met Udo Hirsch. He was rather impressed, and also more than a bit jealous. 'Udo was there with his wife and a friend to help. He had a boat, and all kinds of equipment – Hasselblad cameras and so on. And he was staying three months. I had only four weeks' holiday, which included several days getting to and from Manyas. But the thing that really struck me was that he was making a good living by photographing those birds! I said to myself, "You must be stupid. Why don't you do the same thing yourself?" By then I had seen my own photographs from the year before, and they weren't bad. I thought it must be possible for me to earn a living as a wildlife photographer.'

So the idea was born, and three years later, in 1974, he felt confident enough to take the plunge. He gave up his job with Uniliver and started his first expedition as a full-time professional photographer, a three-month trip to the remote island of Foula in the Shetlands.

Why choose the Shetlands? 'I knew that I had to   7

build up a library of good photographs fairly quickly if I was going to survive in my new career. I already knew something about Foula – I knew of a cottage I could rent – and I anticipated being able to take a lot of pictures of sea birds in a fairly short time.' (The first of Günter's photographs that I ever saw were some splendid pictures of skuas, taken on Foula, which I later published in *Wildlife* magazine.)

Eight months later he was almost broke, but he managed to survive by working as a taxi-driver for several weeks. This extra money made it possible to travel again in 1975 to Scandinavia. Gradually his work was becoming better known, and he could rely on a steady income from his photographs. Thus encouraged, he set off in 1976 on a one-year trip through South America, driving his Volkswagen van from Colombia down to Patagonia.

This trip was not without its problems. 'The animals in South America are certainly more difficult to photograph than those in many other places,' he comments. 'A lot of them are nocturnal, and many species are now rather rare. Before I went, people told me not to waste my time. They said I could not hope to get good wildlife photographs in South America, and that it would be more sensible to go to see them in the best zoos in Europe.'

Despite the difficulties, that journey resulted in a large collection of remarkable photographs, on the strength of which he received an assignment to illustrate a book on the national parks of Peru, which is still his favourite country. Other expeditions have taken him to Ecuador and the Galapagos Islands, the Philippines, Spain, and New Guinea, where he was able to photograph birds of paradise displaying in the wild.

In 1980 Günter met Angelika Hofer, then a zoology student at the University of Munich. They made several short trips together, including one visit to the Netherlands to study and photograph the courtship behaviour of that marvellous bird, the ruff. And this brings the story almost up to date, for in 1981 Angelika graduated with a Bachelor of Science degree, and was free to leave with Günter on an extended expedition to Kenya.

Günter's great dream had always been to visit Africa, inspired perhaps by that book of cigarette cards lent to him by his grandfather during the war. But curiously, that dream had lost some of its intensity after he started working as a wildlife photographer. 'I still longed to see the great herds of plains game, the lions and the cheetahs, and the birds...but I wondered whether I would actually enjoy working in Africa.'

Günter's journey through South America had convinced him that what he enjoyed most, and what enabled him to do his best work, was being in a perfectly natural area, in a wilderness. 'I like to be alone,' he confides, 'or with only one or two other people, and to spend my time looking for the animals. I enjoy waiting for them to appear, and

Camp-site near the balloon pilots' house at Governor's Camp. Angelika sits on the banks of the Mara River, while 'Wendy' (actually a large bull elephant) walks through the trees behind.

sometimes this may take a long time. But Africa is different. In the reserves and parks you have to go out in a vehicle, except in one or two places where you are allowed to walk. And for most of the time you have other people around, other vans and mini-buses, and I don't like that very much.'

He points out that he is not against tourism as such, and he knows that few of the reserves would exist at all without paying visitors. 'But it is a problem for me, as a photographer. I need to concentrate single-mindedly to do my best work, and I am afraid that the presence of other people is distracting. I remember meeting a French photographer who didn't enjoy going out alone, and was always looking for someone to go with him. I am not like that at all. I am happiest when I am working on my own, when I see nobody at all! I do not include Angelika in this, of course, because she is interested in the same things as I am. She wants to find and observe the wildlife, not other human beings. She doesn't want to talk all the time, and she is happy with the routine involved in getting up very early and then perhaps spending many hours waiting for something to happen.'

There was another thing that made him less eager to work in Africa than in some other places he had been: the fact that it was a fairly well-trodden route. 'There was another German photographer, Reinhard Kürkel, who had spent ten years in Kenya and Tanzania. There were Alan Root, the Bartletts, Hugo van Lawick, and others — and they had taken some of their best pictures when it was rather easier than it is now.'

Nevertheless, Günter felt that he had to go sooner or later. Besides, he wanted to see Africa for himself. 'I did not necessarily expect to bring back a spectacular series of photographs, but I did want to see what I could do. I suppose that in a way I wanted to compare what I could do with the work of others who had been before me.'

Günter and Angelika chose to concentrate on Kenya, partly because they reckoned it would be more convenient to work in than other countries, and partly because of the range of different habitats — plains, mountains, lakes, and forests — all within a comparatively small area.

Knowing that they would need transport, they decided to buy a vehicle in Germany and ship it to Mombasa, rather than to buy one out there, which would have been equally easy. The main reason was comfort. 'In Nairobi we would only be able to buy a standard vehicle, but to allow ourselves the maximum freedom — and a more comfortable life — we wanted to equip it in advance.'

So they bought a VW van, similar to the mini-buses that are such a familiar feature of the East African parks, and fitted it out with a bed, a gas cooker, and a fridge. Another advantage of shipping the van from Germany by sea was that they could pack it with a lot of extra equipment — things like photographic hides and heavy tripods — at no extra cost.

'The van did not have four-wheel-drive,' says Günter, 'and we were warned that this might give us some problems. The choice was, therefore, our comfortable van, or a four-wheel-drive vehicle,

The photographs in this book were all taken in the parks and reserves of Kenya on this map.

10

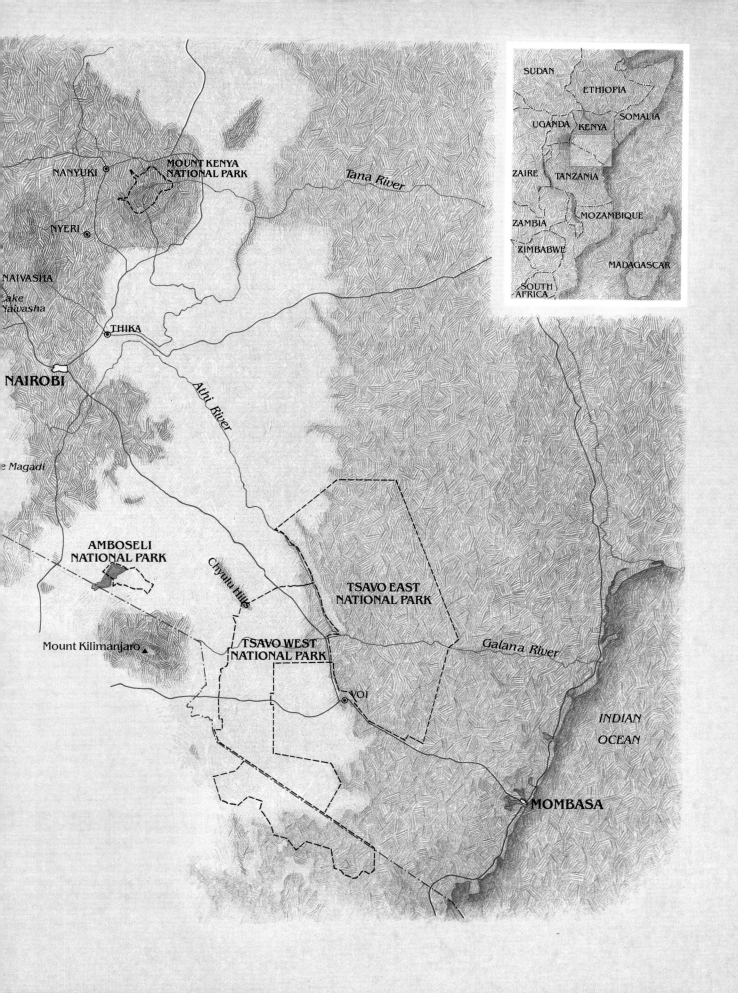

something like a Land-Rover or a Toyota. We chose comfort, and I think we made the right choice. Occasionally we had to stay in camp when it was raining and the tracks were too slippery, but we were in the Masai Mara for five months altogether, and we lost only a very few days because of this.'

The advantage of their well-equipped van was its convenience as much as its comfort. They did not need hotels or lodges, or even a tent. They could cook for themselves and stay where they wanted (which, of course, meant recognized camp-sites inside the parks and reserves). As Günter puts it, 'All we had to do was buy a lot of food and be on our way. And in the reserves we could be very flexible. For example, I need my breakfast in the morning ...but cooking in the van only took a few minutes, and we could still be away before sunrise, or even in the dark. In the middle of the day we could stay where we were, and didn't have to return to the camp-site or lodge for lunch. If we were watching some cheetahs, for example, we could just stay there and eat our meal while we waited.'

As to the trip itself, they had little difficulty planning where to go as there was plenty of published information about Kenya.

They decided to go out to Kenya in August 1981, and stay for six months. Then they would leave for a while, because in Günter's experience they would need a break after this length of time, if not before. Furthermore, they would not be able to take enough film to last much longer. 'We had about 300 rolls of film for six months,' says Günter. 'That is not very much. Normally I would use that amount in three months.'

Most of the film was Kodachrome 64, with some rolls of Ektachrome for poor light conditions. In fact, they did not take all of the film with them, storing most of it with friends in Nairobi, and taking only what they needed for each excursion. From time to time other friends would carry exposed film back to Germany for processing.

They were surprised and delighted with the Masai Mara, the first reserve they visited in Kenya. 'We did not know about the wildebeest crossing points on the Mara River (see pages 182-93), nor did we know where there are lions that hunt in the daytime, or where hyenas accept cars close to their den.

Just before Günter and Angelika reached the Masai Mara, on the first of their three visits, they met a man who asked where they were going and then offered his services as a guide. 'But he was too expensive for us,' recalls Günter. 'Most people, of course, only go for a day or two, but we were going for a month or six weeks, and could not possibly afford to take a guide with us for so long. However, as part of his sales pitch, he told us about some of the best places to go. For example, he told us we should go to the western part of the reserve, near Governor's Camp, and not to the other end. We

Günter prepares to photograph a lion cub in the vast expanse of the plains of the Masai Mara.

would probably have discovered this sooner or later, but he saved us a lot of time. Maybe meeting that man was our first piece of good luck!'

As I mentioned at the beginning of this introduction, 'luck' in wildlife photography tends to flow more towards the expert than the beginner. This is not a question of those who need it the least getting the most. It happens because the expert goes about things in such a way as to be better placed to take advantage of any lucky breaks that may arise. The ordinary tourist visiting Kenya may well have the good fortune to witness a lion kill, or come upon a hyena suckling her cubs. But Günter Ziesler and others like him are far more likely to see such events – for several good reasons.

Günter and Angelika travelled through Kenya for a year, compared with the fortnight or so that most visitors spend there (and many of them divide even those two weeks between the national parks and the beaches on the coast). They would often set out from their camp-site before dawn, so as to be in position near some animals that they wanted to photograph before sunrise. This is the best time of day to be out watching wildlife, but unfortunately many of the safari drivers are reluctant to be up so early – an attitude that may have been at least partly fostered by the fact that many tourists do not care to rise early either, because they are 'on holiday'.

Günter and Angelika were frequently prepared to stay beside a group of animals, perhaps a lion pride or some cheetahs, or a group of hyenas, waiting for something to happen. Sometimes half or even a whole day might pass in this way. This is a luxury denied to the tourist with limited time, of course, and if such a proposal were to be made by someone on a Kenya safari, it is not hard to imagine the reaction of fellow-passengers in the mini-bus! Günter's experience on other wildlife photographic expeditions and Angelika's zoological knowledge undoubtedly gave them an edge in being able to predict what might happen in a given situation, or where and when to position themselves to the best advantage.

Finally, in addition to equipping the inside of their van with creature comforts, Günter brought a small tripod that he was able to fit to the driver's door. This gave a good, steady support for his camera, and although it meant that he was only able to photograph out of one side, this was not a big problem since he was normally driving himself, and could position the van wherever he wanted. While many safari drivers do their best to be helpful, it is impossible for them to know exactly when to stop, where to turn, and so forth. But Günter, being both driver and photographer, had total control over the positioning of his mobile hide.

I mention these points not only to explain in part how Günter came to take such superb photographs, but also by way of consolation to anyone who has already been on such a safari and is not wholly satisfied with the photographic results. And to those who have yet to go, my advice is to enjoy the experience to the maximum, at the time, and not to pin all hopes on bringing back pictures like the ones to be seen in this book. I have travelled about as widely as Günter, though not for such extended periods, and I have learned to accept my limitations as a photographer.

Reading Angelika's diaries, it occurred to me that some of the time they spent waiting for something to happen might have been rather boring. It is, after all, no more exciting to watch a lion sleeping for three hours than it is for half an hour! But if a photographer is not prepared to sit through the more tedious times, he runs the risk of missing the moments of action.

Patience is probably the most important attribute of a wildlife photographer, or indeed of anyone who wants to observe animals and find out more about their way of life. The endurance that Günter and Angelika displayed on their Kenya safari was amply rewarded with many telling observations of animal behaviour. They watched many lion hunts, for example, and it is interesting to hear how many of these were not successful. It is notable, too, how young and inexperienced lions can spoil a hunt for their elders by advancing at the wrong moment. Lions, like all animals, have to learn. Lions are especially fascinating animals to watch because, unlike other cats, they are social creatures and often hunt communally. I was particularly struck by Angelika's account of the occasion when they watched one lioness follow a wart hog, driving it literally into the jaws of another lioness that lay hidden in some long grass.

Some behaviour was, at first, harder to interpret. A lioness, and later two hyenas, passed by the carcass of a slender mongoose, but did not attempt to eat it, though one of the hyenas did roll on it. (The dead mongoose apparently produces a powerful smell that deters would-be scavengers.) And then there was the time they saw a young and presumably very low-ranking female hyena being spurned by the other members of her clan, including a six-month-old cub.

Their eyes were not always on the ground, and there was much for them to watch among the birds; nest-building by a pair of Verreaux's eagles, for instance, and the busy courtship of weaver birds, not to mention the curious nesting behaviour of different species of hornbills. While Günter tended to concentrate his camera on the mammals, it is worth emphasizing that the savannahs of East Africa have a particularly rich birdlife.

They also had the opportunity to observe the behaviour of some of their fellow visitors to the parks. One stationary vehicle will often attract others because there may be something interesting going on. This can lead to a circle of mini-buses forming round a group of animals – which do not always enjoy such close attention. Once they saw a python that had temporarily abandoned its newly killed prey because a vehicle had driven too close. And on another occasion a cheetah gave up her attempt at a hunt because she was distracted by onlookers.

Most drivers know what they should or should not do, but they are in a difficult position, having also to try to please their passengers. They could well find it difficult to refuse a full load of camera-laden 13 passengers, who want to get closer because they do not have telephoto lenses or binoculars. The problem used to be particularly acute in Amboseli, where cheetahs were forced to hunt at night because of daytime disturbance, though things have improved there since vehicles have been obliged to stay on the tracks.

On a related matter, it may probably be noticed while this book is being read that little or no mention is made concerning wildlife conservation. This is deliberate, because the main point is to convey the rich drama of the daily lives of Kenya's wild animals through text and pictures. This book is not intended to be about conservation itself — though, if it succeeds in making more people understand more about wildlife, it will surely increase their sympathy towards conservation ideas. Günter and Angelika, and indeed all of us who have been associated with this book, realize that animals and their habitats are seriously threatened, in Kenya as elsewhere. Two animals in particular come to mind in this respect: the elephant and the rhino, which are still being slaughtered illegally for their tusks and horns.

There is one other aspect of the production of *Safari* that requires comment. With literally hundreds of photographs from which to choose, and diaries covering the best part of a year, some editorial selectivity was necessary. The photographs speak for themselves, but having been involved in the initial choice, I can say with assurance that there were many, many more that we could have used, but for which there was no space. We decided not to caption the photographs selected, but rather let the diary entries explain the scenes and events shown. A small number within the border of each photograph keys into the diary text. With regard to the text, some observations — indeed, some whole days — were omitted either to avoid undue repetition of similar happenings, or in some cases simply because nothing of great interest took place. Otherwise, the text is essentially as Angelika wrote it from day to day.

Although I hinted earlier that we should not be too disappointed if our own pictures do not match those of Günter Ziesler, he does have a few tips to pass on. 'Give yourself maximum freedom and flexibility by hiring your own vehicle, and by camping where possible, instead of using hotels or lodges. Get up early, preferably before sunrise, and take your time exploring the parks. And keep your camera handy and loaded with film at all times, to avoid missing any opportunities. I myself nearly missed some important shots, at Kilaguni Lodge in Tsavo West, when I was in one place and my camera was in another.'

Finally, I asked Günter if he felt they had made any new discoveries during their Kenya safari. 'I don't know whether we discovered anything that is new to science, but we certainly learned many things that were new to us. Everything seems like a discovery when you see it for the first time, with your own eyes!'

Driving along a typical *murram* track in Tsavo West, Kenya's largest national park.

14

ONE

MASAI MARA I

Located in south-western Kenya, on the Tanzanian border, the 645-square-mile Masai Mara National Reserve represents a northern extension of the Serengeti National Park. In fact, the two together form an ecosystem, and during the annual migration the wildebeest (white-bearded gnu), in particular, show no regard for national borders as they cross over into Kenya.

From the edge of the Loita Hills in the east to the Siria Escarpment in the west, the Masai Mara consists of vast rolling plains and rounded hills. The hill-tops are covered with rocks and boulders, scattered trees and bushes, and acacia thornbush.

The Mara River and some of its tributaries, such as the Sand and Talek Rivers, flow throughout the year. Combined with the existence of some marshy areas and scattered rains outside the rainy season, this creates such good conditions that Masai Mara is one of the richest wildlife areas in Kenya.

There are large herds of wildebeest and zebras during the migration period from July to September, and also big populations of lions and hyenas. Cheetahs are easy to observe, though leopards are very shy. The number of elephants is increasing, but only a very few rhinos are left.

Masai Mara was established as a reserve in 1961, and until about a decade ago was covered to a greater extent than now by acacia thornbush. However, the increasing elephant population caused a transformation to more open grassland.

After spending four weeks in Nairobi waiting for our van to arrive from Germany, we were finally able to start our safari on Friday 11 September, 1981. Completing some last-minute shopping in the morning, we left Nairobi at lunch-time.

After a one night stop en route at Narok, we arrived at the western edge of the Mara and camped to watch the sun setting and the moon rising at the same time over the Siria Escarpment.

A thunderstorm builds up over the grasslands of the Mara.

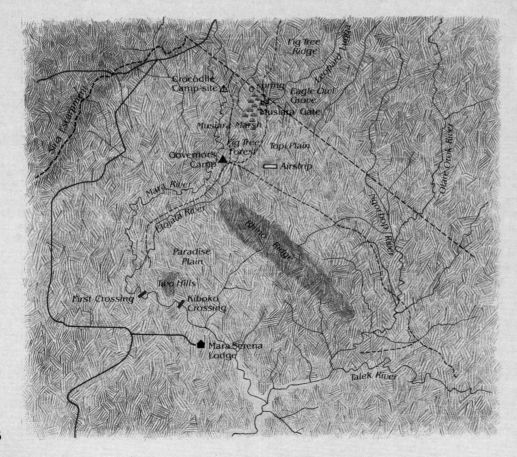

1

SUNDAY 13 SEPTEMBER

We get up before sunrise to see a long line of wildebeest passing us, heading south. Two topi bucks are contesting a territory: the victor pursues his rival for a short distance, then returns to his station on a termite mound.

Leaving the main track we head across country. The plains give way to thick acacia thornbush where herds of topis, zebras, and Grant's gazelles are scattered.

Soon we reach a shallow ravine where rock hyraxes are sunning themselves on the boulders, and fresh elephant dung hints at recent visitors. Crossing the ravine with some difficulty, we stop for lunch under a large tree.

It is not far to the edge of the stony ridge that overlooks the plains. Driving parallel to the ridge, we reach the main track again, enter the reserve, and head for Governor's Camp, a tented camp for tourists.

Governor's Camp has similar facilities to a lodge, but with more of a wilderness feeling. The Game Department has a base here, and we are directed to the football pitch where we can camp.

Keen not to waste any time, we decide to go out for a short game drive for what is left of the afternoon. Soon we are rewarded with a view of three lionesses who killed a wildebeest only 200 yards from the camp. These animals are not part of a pride, but travel on their own as a splinter group. All, however, are offspring of the 'airstrip pride'. Two are sisters, and we call them simply 'the sisters'. The third is a half-sister of the other two, and we call her 'Diana' after the Roman goddess of hunting, for she proves to be an extremely skilful hunter. She is easy to recognize because the tip of her tail is missing.

MONDAY 14 SEPTEMBER

Early in the morning we drive to the wildebeest carcass that Diana and the sisters had killed the day before. At first light the vultures arrive – Ruppell's, white-backed, hooded, and some lappet-faced. Soon they are joined by a black-backed jackal. The lions have not left much so the fight for a piece of bone or fur is fierce, dominated by the jackal who tries to drive the vultures away.

Moving on along the riverine forest, we leave the road and cross to an isolated stand of gallery forest called 'Fig Tree Forest'. Among the trees there are some ponds where water lilies are in flower and two pelicans are feeding. Waterbuck frequent the edge of the forest and the nearby reeds. A blue monkey calls from the top of a tall tree.

1.30pm After lunch we set out along the riverine forest again, this time downstream. To our left a lugga, or dry stream bed, meanders through high grass, its path marked by a few trees and shrubs. Scanning the plains through binoculars, we pick out four cheetahs – a mother and three nearly full-grown cubs – in the shadow of a large tree. Cautiously we make our way through the grass towards them.

2.30pm The female gets up, looks around, and walks towards a small bachelor herd of Grant's gazelles. But they mingle with a large herd of wildebeest before she can get close, so she stops and rests in the grass with her cubs (1).

After about an hour she gets up and continues her walk. Again, the cubs soon follow.

The cheetah heads for a group of Thomson's gazelles (Tommies), but they see her coming and run off. She walks past a mixed herd of zebras and topis that stand and watch her progress, the zebras barking in alarm. But downhill some Grant's gazelles are grazing, unaware of the potential danger.

At a range of about 100 yards the cheetah starts to sprint. The gazelles take flight. She aims for a small fawn – and catches it after a chase of about 300 yards. She leaves the prey for her cubs, but the fawn is still alive and tries to escape (2). The startled cubs seem to hesitate, so their mother has to catch it again. This time it is dead, and within a few minutes has been torn apart by the youngsters.

The mother lies apart from her cubs for at least half an hour, recovering from the exertions of the chase. Then she joins them and starts to feed herself.

2

FRIDAY **18** SEPTEMBER

Early in the morning we go out to look for the lions of the airstrip pride. We meet the two males not far from the airstrip, lazily lying in the grass waiting for the first warming rays of sun. Nothing much is happening so we drive on, up the slope of Rhino Ridge.

Through binoculars we spot the cheetahs again, down in the plain near Governor's Camp. We arrive just in time to watch them hunting.

One of the cubs, a male, tries it first, while his mother and sisters rest in the grass. He stalks a group of Tommies, but he is too eager and advances too fast without looking for cover. The gazelles see him in time and make their getaway.

He returns to the others, and the cubs start to play. As they chase one another they are practising 'stalk', 'ambush', and 'hunt'. But their mother is by now heading for Fig Tree Forest, so they break off and follow. All four cheetahs climb a grassy termite mound and scan the southern end of the marsh. Suddenly the mother vanishes into the reeds. The cubs stay where they are, following her only with their eyes. Then one of them utters a soft whistle and all three run into the marsh.

Their mother has caught a half-grown Tommy. The whole family starts to eat at once, and within half an hour there is little left but a few bones and a piece of fur.

For the rest of the morning the cheetahs stay at the edge of Fig Tree Forest, lying in the shade of the trees.

5.00pm A female cub stalks a group of Grant's gazelles, but she starts her sprint too soon and the gazelles escape. We leave them at about 6.00 pm.

SATURDAY **19** SEPTEMBER

We set out to look for the cheetahs very early in the morning, but fail to find them, so we go instead to the water-filled murram (undersoil) pit at the airstrip.

Here the two sisters are about to stalk a Thomson's gazelle. The two lionesses and the gazelle form a triangle, with the gazelle at the apex. The sisters crouch low in the grass, waiting for the gazelle to come towards them. It does indeed come closer as it grazes, passing within thirty yards of one of them. But she gives up without chasing it, and goes over to one of the grass-clad murram mounds alongside the water-hole and lies down. Perhaps she was disturbed by a car.

The other lioness starts to stalk some more gazelles, but suddenly stops and transfers her attention to a group of zebras that is approaching the water. She is behind them, while her sister is in front of them, at the water-hole. Some of the zebras start to drink, but one is still grazing, standing apart from the others with his back to the stalking lioness. She breaks into a run when she is about fifty yards away, but the zebras stampede in all directions and she misses her prey.

Shortly before noon a big herd of wildebeest approaches the water-hole, but this time some tourists come along and drive close to the lions, forgetting that they might want to hunt. The wildebeest are disturbed, and now avoid the water and the cars.

SUNDAY **20** SEPTEMBER

Once more we set out to look for the cheetahs, but again in vain. Instead we meet Diana and one of the two sisters, trotting from the murram pit water-hole at the airstrip towards Fig Tree Forest. They lie down among some termite mounds near the edge of the forest.

In the distance we can see a herd of wildebeest galloping towards the two lionesses. When they are about 100 yards away they suddenly stop abruptly.

They are very nervous. They sense that ahead of them lies danger: to their right is the forest, and to their left a line of vehicles. The wildebeest start to walk around in a circle, but after half an hour they have calmed down and begin to graze.

Now Diana moves stealthily towards them, and we can only see the tips of her ears when she peers through the grass. When she is twenty yards from the first wildebeest she leaps forward. The wildebeest in front jumps aside and the others scatter. Diana runs from side to side, two more wildebeest manage to escape, then she leaps onto the back of another, bringing it to the ground.

We start the van and drive through the grass as quickly as we can. In the excitement we fail to notice a small termite mound that is right in our path. The van jumps into the air and, as we touch ground again, the 600mm lens I am holding on my knees bounces up and cracks me on the chin.

I realize that I have lost a piece of my front tooth, but for the moment there is no time to examine it.

We are now close to the lioness who has the wildebeest by the throat and is about to *suffocate it. The second lioness arrives at the same time as we do, and starts to nibble at the wildebeest's hind-legs. As soon as it is dead Diana releases the throat and licks the animal's face. Finally she backs off, leaving the other lioness to eat on her own. After a while she grabs it by the neck and drags it to cover.*

7.30am We follow the Mara River upstream to look yet again for the cheetahs. But due to last night's thunderstorm the tracks are quite soft, and we get stuck in the black soil. We have to wait for another car to pull us out, but this does not take long. However, our search is fruitless and we decide to return to the camp-site.

8.50am At the turning to Little Governor's Camp we see some mini-buses parked at the edge of the forest. We drive closer and see a male baboon sitting on a branch with a half-grown impala in front of him (3). He has already opened its belly and now he starts to eat. Other baboons are feeding on the ground, but two more males are in the same tree and are watching him closely. Slowly they approach, and it appears

3

that he is frightened because he drops the impala. A pursuit follows on the ground and the baboons vanish into the forest.

As we drive on we see a large group of female impalas, closely watched over by the buck, staring out at us from the shadow of the trees (4 previous pages).

In the afternoon we go out again to try to locate the cheetahs. A big herd of about 500 buffalos are feeding in the marsh. As we pass the marsh later in the afternoon, on our way back, we pass the group of baboons we saw earlier, moving from the forest to the plain. By the side of the road, sitting on a fallen tree, a male 'look-out' seems unconcerned as we pass (5). Another thunderstorm approaches from the east and we return to the camp-site.

MASAI MARA 1981
FRIDAY **25** SEPTEMBER

In the morning we drive to Paradise Plain. Above the Kikobo Crossing eleven lions, mostly juveniles, sprawl on the ground looking sleepily towards the rising sun. As the sun strengthens they get up one after the other and move in the direction of a herd of wildebeest. But the lions' bellies are round and full, and they merely gather round a small water-hole to drink.

10.10am We drive back to the camp-site and then on to Fig Tree Forest. We have just passed a grassy termite mound when we see a wart hog (wild pig) family — two females and ten one-week-old baby wart hogs (6). The youngsters are making their first excursion out of the den.

The tiny animals whirl around and underneath their mother, who is standing in front of the den with her hind-quarters in the entrance hole. The other female, most probably an older daughter, stays nearby, but behind the termite mound. The young wart hogs soon venture from their mother to their grown-up sister and back again. Some stay near their sister for a while. We watch them until noon, when they return to their den because of the heat. We return to the camp-site for lunch.

In the afternoon we visit the lion sisters for a while, but no prey is around. At about 4.00 pm storm clouds move across and we go back to the camp. Minutes later it starts to rain.

6

MONDAY 28 SEPTEMBER

For the last two days it has been raining so we have had to stay at our camp-site. Many birds have now started to sing, such as a pair of white-browed robin chats that we hear dueting from thick undergrowth. Boubou shrikes and woodland kingfishers can be heard, but are hard to locate. We venture out for brief periods to find that dried-up stream beds have turned into rivers, depressions have become lakes, and meadows are now marshes. Marabou storks and fish eagles are hunting cat-fish where zebras had been grazing only a few days before. Most of the tracks are under water.

Our van is now under a big fig tree, about fifty yards from the Mara River and near the Balloon House, a wooden structure on stilts where the balloon pilots live (hot air balloon rides are a tourist attraction in the Mara). We are on a bend in the river, with a steep bank on our side. Around us there is woodland.

Today a pair of cinnamon-chested bee-eaters are starting to excavate their nest-hole in the river bank near the Balloon House. We sit and watch. They do not dig continuously, and spend a lot of time on a branch that overhangs the bank. The male flies into the air, catches a bee which he then bangs against the branch to kill it, and offers it to the female (7).

A pair of Ross's turacos — large, dark violet-coloured birds — cross the river frequently to feed in a fig tree near the Balloon House. On this side of the river they enter the territory of a pair of Schalow's turacos — all-green birds of the same family. They are busily feeding too, and whenever the two species meet, the Schalow's chase the Ross's back to the other side of the river. When these turacos are in flight we can see their flight feathers shining crimson against the blue sky.

Before sunrise we leave for the hyena den above the marsh.

6.30am The den is in a black-earth termite mound. Cubs of every age, from four weeks (when they are still black) to half-grown, wander about in front of the den. 'Eve', the mother of the black twins, lies in the entrance hole, with 'Pregnant', 'Square', and 'Split' nearby. All told there are some twenty females and young hyenas around the den.

8.00am An adult hyena passes the den chasing three topis. Some of the hyenas we are watching leave the den to follow her up the ridge. We follow too, but when we reach the top the hunt seems to have been abandoned and most of the hyenas are lying in a muddy pool among the stones at the edge of the ridge.

Pregnant, an old female with hardly any fur who looks as if she is about to give birth very soon, returns to the den and we follow. At the den we find Eve and the twins, and Square.

Although this is our first visit to the den, we can soon identify many of the hyenas and give them names; most of them have distinct ear marks (probably the result of fights).

SUNDAY **4** OCTOBER

Today we are at the hyena den before sunrise.

6.30am Split, Eve, and the twins are at the den, with several other animals nearby. The twins are playing 'catch-me' with a juvenile. 'Point' arrives and is greeted by both the twins and the juvenile.

6.50am Suddenly all the adult hyenas set out and head for the ridge. First they follow the course of a stream bed until they reach its northern end, where twenty-six of them gather and move on together up the ridge. Their tails are raised aggressively as they run across the stony plateau.

Ten hyenas stop by a clump of grass, sniff, begin to dig, urinate, and then one after another mark the grass with scent from glands under their tails. Some yards away we see some bloody marks on the ground and the grassy stomach contents of an antelope. The hyenas inspect the surroundings very closely, and twice more we see them marking clumps of grass.

They continue for another 100 yards or so before they stop and stare into the distance for a while. Then they all turn around and run back the way they have come. We assume that hyenas of another clan had entered the territory of our clan and killed a wildebeest. Our hyenas had heard them and went out to defend their territory. Failing to find the intruders, they marked their territory instead.

TUESDAY **6** OCTOBER

Most of the hyenas, except for the twins, leave the den just before sunrise. We follow two juveniles which go in the direction of Musiara Gate. They meet Pregnant and two young-sters on the hill near the gate.

On our way back to camp we stay for a while with three young male giraffes at the edge of the marsh. They are fighting playful-ly, striking out with their long necks and butting their opponents on the flanks and legs with their little horns. Sometimes two of them will intertwine their necks, which is quite a comical sight (8). The fighting is clearly not very serious, as it soon stops and the giraffes carry on grazing peacefully. We leave them and return to the camp.

MASAI MARA 1981

THURSDAY **8** OCTOBER

Today we look in vain for hyenas at the den. Later we discover that Eve and her twins, as well as Pregnant and five new females, are at a new den, more than 500 yards east of the original one.

We stay with the hyenas all day, watching some interesting behaviour.

There must have been a fight, though we didn't see it, for one of the hyenas comes running back to the den with a bleeding ear. She retreats to lie in a muddy pool.

In the afternoon the activity starts quite early. One female vomits near the den and all the cubs gather to roll in it.

FRIDAY **9** OCTOBER

7.00am Today we arrive later than usual at the hyena den. Eve, her twins, and some other adults are there.

7.30am Some wildebeest are grazing on the hill above the murram pit water-hole near Musiara Gate. Suddenly we notice a calf running downhill towards the lugga, a hyena at his heels. She had managed to separate it from the rest of the herd, but the calf is now heading for a group of zebras at the foot of the hill. It gets among the zebras, whereupon the hyena stops and appears to abandon the chase.

However, the zebras become nervous and gallop away, leaving the calf exposed once more. Seeing its chance, the hyena follows and forces the young wildebeest towards the marsh. As they pass by the den the other hyenas take notice (9) and one of them joins

the hunt. Again and again the calf turns to look back at its pursuers. Now four more hyenas, which have been resting on the hill, run down and join the others.

We follow in the van, but cautiously, remembering the accident when I lost part of my tooth.

After about one mile the first hyena catches the calf by the tail. It is soon on the ground. At this moment we arrive on the scene.

The hyenas seem to be very hungry. They gnaw at its legs and open up its stomach, even before the calf is dead (10). More hyenas come from every direction. We notice that only the adults are eating, while the younger animals stand around and wait, with a Ruppell's vulture, hoping for a chance to snatch a morsel. Soon an old female hyena arrives and chases off nearly all the others.

Two manage to steal a leg and run, chased by some others. A juvenile gets hold of the tail. Two jackals appear, but wait at a safe distance. The hyenas which have eaten enough move away and sprawl on the ground, merely lifting their bloody heads occasionally to watch the action.

Forty minutes later only the head and a piece of skin are left, which the dominant female leaves to her cub.

We return to the camp-site.

We leave Governor's Camp at 11.00am the next day, driving across wide plains with big herds of wildebeest to Keekorok Lodge. After two more days, at the Sand River Camp, we finally leave Masai Mara for Nairobi.

TWO

AMBOSELI

Amboseli National Park is located on Kenya's southern border, north-west of the highest mountain in Africa, Mount Kilimanjaro, whose snow-capped peak dominates the scenery.

The park takes its name from Lake Amboseli, a saline and generally dry lake bed that is only seasonally flooded. The climate is mostly hot and dry. Though much of the lake basin is very flat, there are some prominent volcanic hills in the south and a varied landscape of open plains, acacia woodland, lava-strewn thornbush, and some permanent swamps and marshes supporting sedges and papyrus.

There are large herds of elephants and a rich bird life. The park is very popular with tourists, however, and lions and cheetahs, in particular, have suffered from disturbance while hunting. In past years the vegetation has been damaged by over-grazing by Masai cattle and tourist vehicles driving across country. Now vehicles are strictly prohibited from leaving the tracks.

To the north of Amboseli lie the Chyulu Hills, a compact range of volcanic origin some thirty miles in length. The highest point is 7,200 feet above sea level. Despite frequent rain showers, the moisture quickly seeps through the porous lava and cinder, so there is virtually no permanent water and thus no human inhabitants. But the hills support patches of lush, evergreen mist forest and a good variety of wildlife.

After two weeks in Nairobi we set off for Amboseli on Friday 23 October, 1981, and arrived at our camp-site by late afternoon.

A wonderful view of Kilimanjaro and giraffes standing between the fever trees (yellow-barked acacias).

SATURDAY 24 OCTOBER

7.30am After breakfasting we drive back to the main road and turn off in the direction of Amboseli Serena Lodge. The track runs along the eastern edge of a forest that borders a swamp. There has been no rain for a long time and all the grass is very short or burnt. The clouds of dust give one the impression of being in a desert. We have a magnificent view of Mount Kilimanjaro, which is completely free of clouds, even the top, where we can see a small cap of snow.

8.15am Before reaching the lodge we turn off to the right and follow another track, which keeps us by the forest and the swamp. The forest vegetation is dominated by fever trees and palm trees.

We encounter a small herd of elephants accompanied by cattle egrets. The elephants are breaking off acacia branches and eating them, regardless of the long, sharp thorns. A cow elephant stands with her tiny calf in the middle of the track. The calf is so small that it can easily walk about beneath its mother, and seems to show little interest in her feeding activity.

Along the way we meet a number of lone elephant bulls, as well as zebras, wildebeest, impalas, and Thomson's gazelles.

4.30pm We have hardly arrived back at the camp-site when the vervet monkeys start to leave the acacias where they have been feeding on the fresh young shoots and thorns (11). They can be very mischievous and one can't afford to take one's eyes off them for a moment. But they are amusing to watch, and we enjoy their company for the rest of the afternoon. They sit on top of the van and look through the windows. We set up a barbecue for our evening meal and temporarily forget about the monkeys — whereupon we promptly lose our dinner when one of them snatches the meat from the fire!

11

34

SUNDAY 25 OCTOBER

7.00am Soon after sunrise we set out for Olokenya Swamp, a big marshy area to the east of our camp-site. First we drive along the main road towards the park's Kimana Gate. Beside the road there is a herd of grazing elephants, and we stop to watch as two young bulls push against one another in a trial of strength (12).

Then we drive on and turn off the road to encircle the swamp. The contrast between semi-desert on one side of the track and thick vegetation on the other is very striking. Large mixed herds of wildebeest and zebra graze on the short grass. We see some kori bustards and two-banded coursers – typical birds of the semi-desert.

10.20am Having completed our circuit of the swamp we continue towards the Amboseli Serena Lodge and take the same track as yesterday. On the edge of the forest we stop to watch a Kirk's dik-dik (a very small antelope) that is hiding in the shrubby undergrowth.

After a while the dik-dik comes out, but does not look in our direction: instead, it stares into the bushes. We follow its gaze and, although it is hidden from the dik-dik, we can see a leopard crouching behind a bush only ten yards from the little antelope. The dik-dik's curiousity aroused, it slowly advances towards the leopard which waits silently. But then, just at the moment when the leopard starts to pounce, the dik-dik turns and races away. We return to the camp-site for lunch.

3.35pm This afternoon we drive along the swamp again to Observation Hill. We meet a driver there who tells us that he has just been to the end of the swamp, where a rock python has caught a Thomson's gazelle and is beginning to eat it.

12

4.10pm We arrive at the site of the kill, but can only see the gazelle -- an adult female — by the edge of the water. Then we spot the python. It must be about ten feet long, and is lying curled up in the grass nearby. Judging by the tyre marks, the other cars had stopped about three feet from the snake — which was far too close.

Keeping at a sensible distance (not so much from the point of view of safety, but in order not to disturb the snake unduly), we stop the van and wait. Before long the snake lifts its head cautiously and with its tongue flicking in and out looks for its prey. Very slowly it approaches the gazelle, gliding along the carcass, apparently investigating the contours with its tongue until it discovers the head.

The snake's mouth opens and it grips the head, simultaneously making a coil around the gazelle's head, just at the base of the horns. Muscles ripple beneath its skin as it tightens its grip. After ten, perhaps twenty seconds of maximum effort the horns break with a loud crack (13). Now the python begins to swallow. After about an hour the head, including the loose, hanging horns, disappear down the snake's throat (14). Progress is now faster for a while, as it is not very hard to get down the slender neck. But then come the shoulders and the front legs. The great jaws — that in snakes are not joined together — open very wide (15), and ever so slowly inch forwards, pausing from time to time for breaks of several minutes. Now the python makes a second coil round the gazelle's body to give it greater purchase. By squeezing the prey, the snake stretches it somewhat, which makes it easier to swallow (16). The skin around the snake's head and neck has stretched by three- or four-fold. It looks as if it will tear apart under the strain. Unfortunately, it is beginning to get dark and we have to leave before the python has completely swallowed its prey.

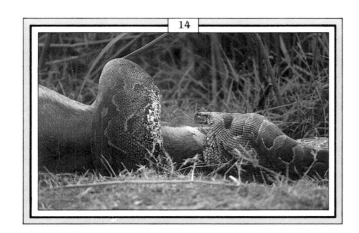

MONDAY 26 OCTOBER

6.30am We go straight to the swamp to look for the rock python, but it has gone and there is no sign of yesterday's drama.

We then drive back along the swamp and into the forest. Here we come across the male dik-dik again and watch it for a while. It grazes under a bush, and here and there it marks a grass stem with its eye-gland (17). Then it retreats under another bush and lies down.

We continue along the swamp until we reach its western end, where we turn and drive back along the other side. We encounter

17

a large herd of buffalos mixed with wildebeest and elephants, all grazing in the reeds. It is a lovely sight, with cattle egrets riding on the backs of the buffalos and elephants, and walking about between the legs of the wildebeest, Mount Kilimanjaro providing a fitting backdrop.

We drive on until we come to an open stretch of water fringed with a few dead trees. Some cormorants and a fish eagle sit in the branches. A flock of white-faced tree ducks rests on the shore. The fishing is obviously good here, for we also see yellow-billed and saddle-bill storks, and goliath and grey herons. A tiny, brilliant blue malachite kingfisher perches at the top of a reed stem (18).

We continue to reach an area of dry bush. Somewhere in the distance is Lake Amboseli, but although the track continues along the swamp we cannot go any farther for fear of getting stuck in the mud. We stop for lunch in the shade of a big acacia. No sooner have we come to a halt than about 100 elephants appear out of the bush. Half-concealed in a cloud of dust, they march off towards the papyrus swamps of Lake Amboseli.

When we get underway again in the afternoon we discover a rhino that had been lying in a muddy pool only 100 yards from where we stopped for lunch. It has a large calf that stays in the bushes. Unfortunately, we cannot enjoy this spectacle for long as an elephant drives the rhino away.

On returning to our camp-site we build a big fire and savour the evening.

TUESDAY 27 OCTOBER

This morning we head once more for the western end of the swamp, and stop by a small water-hole.

8.30am We watch flocks of chestnut-bellied sandgrouse arrive (19 overleaf). When the birds take to the air again, they do so with a loud noise produced by their rapid wing-flapping. The sandgrouse come and go for more than an hour.

We leave to have a look for the rhino, but without success. When we come back the water-hole is full of wildebeest, which are on their way to the plains.

In the afternoon we drive around the Olokenya Swamp. Near Ol Tukai Lodge we explore the open grassland.

5.10pm When a number of vehicles gather together it means that something interesting is going on. It turns out that a rhino with a calf is being watched (20). The mother is rather shy and nervous, and tries to escape from the circle of cars. But she calms down when these eventually move on so that some lions nearby may be observed. We spend the rest of the day with the rhino, which soon starts to browse.

20

WEDNESDAY 28 OCTOBER

Today we drive out from our camp-site and go along the forest. A herd of wildebeest and zebras, accompanied by cattle egrets, grazes between dead trees. Elephants are gradually destroying the forest, and we see many dead trees as we drive in this part of the park.

We join the track along the swamp, just where the Kirk's dik-dik has its territory. This time we find the female, hiding in the undergrowth. On the way back to the camp-site three bull elephants cross in front of us.

2.20pm We are just about to set off after lunch when we discover a big herd of about seventy elephants quite close to our camp (21). They walk through a small marshy area that borders the camp-site. We manage to find a track and follow them for the whole afternoon.

It is interesting to watch them change colour from grey to black as they bathe in the

muddy pools. A large flock of cattle egrets accompanies these great grey – or black – figures, often landing on the backs of the elephants. We also see a buffalo besieged by egrets as it rests in a pool (22).

The cattle egret is now found in many parts of the world, but the species probably originated in this part of Africa. Its preferred breeding habitat is the short grass margins of lakes, marshes, rivers, and especially flood-plains subject to periodic flooding and drying out. Though the egret feeds mainly in the water during the breeding season, it becomes a dry-land feeder at other times. It is then that it is found in characteristic association with large herbivores, especially buffalos. The egrets benefit from the large number of insects stirred up as the animals walk, but they do not feed on ticks or other parasites. In recent years the cattle egret has spread in the Americas in spectacular fashion.

We drive to the end of the track beside the marsh to wait for the elephants. But they don't stay in the marsh as we thought they would. Instead, they start moving in our direction, and before we know what has happened we are surrounded by elephants. Günter takes a shot of a cow nursing her calf (23), and then we close the windows. The elephants pass on without bothering us.

6.20pm Just before sunset the elephants enter the marsh again, and suddenly their grey forms are touched with red and gold by the sinking sun (24). The egrets take wing and fly to their roosting trees. We head back to our own camp-site.

This morning there is mist hanging over the ground. A big herd of buffalos walks past our camp-site, and there is a group of impalas grazing nearby. We take the track that leads to the swamp, and see the dik-diks again. This time we see the whole family – male, female, and a juvenile.

We spend the middle of the day at the camp-site, and at 2.00pm, about the same time as yesterday, the trumpeting of elephants announces their presence in the marsh. Today we approach closer as the wind is in the right direction. We watch them bathing in the muddy water.

24

4.00pm *The sky is cloudy and it begins to drizzle, so we stay at the camp-site. Two lions pay us a visit, but after a short time they move on so that we can sit by the camp fire in the evening.*

FRIDAY 30 OCTOBER

Today we follow the track along the forest, but this time we branch off to take a different route that leads into the forest. We come across the remains of a dead elephant, its skin lying like a shrunken, empty wrapping beside the scattered bones.

At noon we return to the camp-site, and on the way we can see the top of Kilimanjaro above the clouds. It has snowed up there, for the white cap is noticeably bigger.

2.00pm Once again the elephants arrive in the marsh at the camp-site. We follow them in the van.

Some giraffes are browsing, and we notice that one of the males is following a female very closely.

Yellow-billed oxpeckers walk about on their backs searching for ticks and flies.

SATURDAY 31 OCTOBER

This morning a taveta golden weaver joins us for breakfast. This is generally a rather rare bird, but it is quite common in Amboseli, especially at the breakfast table.

Our plan today is to drive to the Chyulu Hills and thence to Tsavo National Park. But before we leave Amboseli we take a short trip along the edge of the forest.

8.10am We have not progressed very far when we encounter the pair of giraffes that we saw yesterday evening. We stay with them for a while, and watch them mating three times (25). As we had seen before, the male is following the female very closely, trying to keep pace with her. Occasionally he touches her neck, thus guiding where she walks. Then he mounts her just before he develops an erection. During copulation both of them continue walking, as only in this way can the female withstand the weight of the male. Several yellow-billed oxpeckers perching on their necks take fright and fly off.

9.00am We finally leave, driving north from Ol Tukai and passing through the Nyeri Desert where for the first time we see some gerenuks (long-necked antelopes) that are well adapted to this kind of semi-desert.

After about eighteen miles we reach Leme Boti Gate. We turn off to the left and drive to Makutano, shown as a village on the map, but in reality only a few huts. From here a secondary road should lead us to the northern end of the Chyulu Range. It seems more like a cattle trail than a road. We pass two Masai villages and then on to a plain, and towards a series of rounded, grass-clad hills that rise to more than 7,000 feet in front of us.

Suddenly an eland crosses in front of us — this is an antelope that is bigger than a domestic cow but a lot more graceful. The hills are getting closer now, a compact range running from north-west to south-east, some forty-five miles north-east of Kilimanjaro.

We pass by twin hills and are at the foot of the main range. Here the dominant vegetation is acacia thornbush of various species. Large groups of kongoni, or Coke's hartebeest (large antelope) (26 overleaf), as well as fringe-eared oryx and Thomson's gazelles, run away from the van, leaving the shade of the acacias and going out onto the plain. The track snakes back and forth as it climbs the ancient cinder cones, which rise here to about 6,000 feet. There are also a few giraffes, but since few vehicles come this way they too are very shy

49

compared with those we have observed in the national parks.

Eventually we leave the bush zone at about 3,500 feet and reach the grasslands. Here there are colourful red-flowering Erythrina trees growing singly or in groups on the grass-clad slopes of the old volcanoes (27). The craters of these volcanoes sometimes contain small islands of forest, varying in size from one to sixty acres (28). Their growth is limited by periodic fires. A few more Erythrina trees are scattered through the forests.

Between the main volcanic craters and the subsidiary cones are some substantial lava flows of various types.

The track clings to the hill-sides, continually taking us down into valleys and up again on the other side. Sometimes, when we are on

27

the western side, we can see across the Loitokitok Plain with its scattered kopjes (out-crops of boulders) to Kilimanjaro rising in the distance.

We pass a hill that clearly illustrates the origin of the range. Instead of a peak, it has a deep crater with a fissure in the south-east wall. Shrubs and grasses have gained a foothold on the volcanic cinder flanks. We climb up to the crater rim. On the edge there are some aloes in flower, while inside there is thick forest. Some of the craters in the Chyulus are 400 to 500 feet deep, and this is one of them.

The forest in these craters depends on the amount of surface erosion and disintegration of volcanic cinder, combined with mist. This action produces soil on the crater walls.

We stop for lunch at the foot of the volcano and then drive on.

Finally we reach the top of a hill at about 6,000 feet, along which we can drive. For the first time we get a view of Kibwezi Plain to the east of the range. After a while the track leads down into a valley again. A buffalo comes out of a forest beside the track.

Sometimes we can only guess where the track leads when it vanishes into the high grass, but somehow we manage to stay on it. Eventually we reach a long valley nestling

between the surrounding hills. To the left is a patch of forest, and we decide to stop here for the night.

Günter explores the forest and finds the bones of an elephant. Creepers and climbing plants hang down from the trees that are also host to many small orchids, some of which are in flower.

We see a speckled mousebird perching on a small bush at the edge of the forest (29). The mousebird's toes and claws are well adapted to climbing among branches. The name is appropriate and is derived from its rodent-like scuttling through the branches with its long tail pointed downwards. We also catch a glimpse of a pair of Hartlaub's turacos building a nest.

As evening draws near, the last rays of the sun bathe the grasslands in gold and the Erythrina trees glow fiery-red. Then we are enclosed by the sounds of the night – the calls of crickets, frogs, and nightjars.

CHYULU HILLS 1981

SUNDAY **1** NOVEMBER

We get up when the first weak sunlight touches our van. It is quite cold outside and we can hardly see through the windows, which are wet with dew. As the sun rises, clouds of mist creep over the hill-tops and flow down into our valley, covering everything with moisture.

In the northern part of the Chyulu Hills there is only one permanent spring. According to local legend there used to be more springs here in former times, when the Wachagga tribe lived here. But when the Wachagga were driven away by the Masai they bewitched the springs, causing them to dry up.

The Chyulus are very wet, due to the regular morning mists and extensive rains during the rainy season, but cinder and lava are very porous and so the rain water quickly seeps away. In fact, it leaves the Chyulus Hills altogether, coming out of the earth again in Tsavo National Park, where Mzima Springs, for example, owe their existence to this water source.

10.00am We finally start, driving at first along a track bordered by flowering Leonotis and high, golden grass. After a while the track leads down to a patch of forest that we have to cross. But we find that we have to cut our way through as the track is overgrown. The trees create a dense green canopy above us, with many epiphytic plants hanging from the tree tops.

We decide to stop here for the rest of the day and the night, and set out to explore the

forest. Numerous birds are singing, including a pair of turacos and some sunbirds. All the time we can hear cicadas.

The sunbirds prefer to visit the Leonotis blossoms that occur outside the forest, but there are many other flowers in bloom.

In the late afternoon we hear some new voices in the forest. A troop of white-throated guenons (monkeys) passes above our heads, probably looking for ripe figs.

In the evening we light a fire beneath our roof of hanging plants. It is almost like being in a circus or gymnasium, among a mass of dangling ropes. We go to bed and can hear loud calls of hyraxes in the tree-tops.

MONDAY **2** NOVEMBER

In the morning we continue driving, but soon come to the Great Chyulu Forest, which is one of the last surviving examples of evergreen cloud forest in Kenya. We stop and explore.

Leaving the track, we follow a game trail, probably created by wild boar or buffalo. It starts to get wet. The mist condenses on the leaves in the tree-tops, and falls down on us like drizzle. Also above us are tangled, moss-covered lianas. But we have to remind ourselves not to spend too much time looking upwards, as there is always the danger of meeting a buffalo. The chance of an encounter here is high, and we have to keep an eye on the next tree we can climb, just in case...

We keep on climbing upwards, using the numerous game trails. We pass giant fig trees wrapped in mist and drizzle. Finally we reach the top, a flat plateau the size of a football field. But the undergrowth here is extremely thick and we have to use buffalo trails, singing loudly and hoping that any buffalo that is around will decide to leave before we arrive.

On the way back we take another trail and come upon an enormous fig tree whose base is about forty feet in diameter (30 overleaf). The tree's 'trunk' consists of a maze of aerial roots that have formed new columnar trunks.

Carrying on downwards we come to a clearing where we frighten away some wild boar, or perhaps a buffalo. Finally we reach the track about a mile from where we started.

We walk back to the van and get underway, as we want to reach Tsavo National Park today.

THREE

TSAVO WEST

Located approximately half-way between Nairobi and the coastal city of Mombasa, Tsavo National Park is Kenya's largest protected area at over 8,000 square miles. It is bisected by the Nairobi-Mombasa road and railway, which for a distance divide the park into Tsavo East and Tsavo West. Much of the former is very arid, with only limited facilities for visitors. The comparatively well-watered Tsavo West attracts most tourists, though it, too, is rather dry. Large game animals are not plentiful, and the park has suffered from over-browsing, especially by elephants. The birdlife, however, is very rich and varied with — among much else — numerous birds of prey and no less than eight species of hornbills.

At the foot of the Chyulu Hills stands a black cinder cone and heaps of red lava. It is Shaitani Volcano, and from it runs a great flow of lifeless lava stretching ten miles into Tsavo National Park. *Pausing on our drive from the Chyulus, on Monday 2 November, we climbed up to have a look at Shaitani's crater. The only signs of life were some lichens and a few grasses that had managed to find a foothold. But the view was splendid — of the Chyulus and Kilimanjaro, and the plains of Tsavo.*

It was already 6.00pm, so we climbed down and made our way towards the park's Chyulu Gate, and the camp-site just outside. This boasted some showers, and we were glad to wash away the dust. It was much warmer that night than it had been up in the hills.

Night falls on Tsavo West, with a lone baobab tree in the foreground and distant Kilimanjaro in the background.

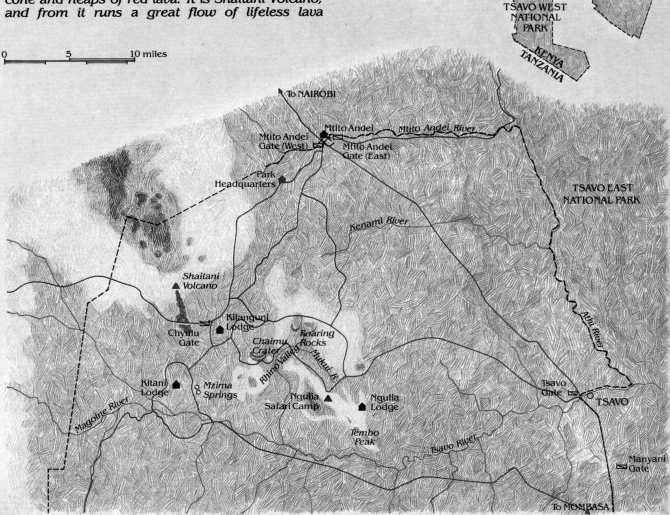

0   5   10 miles

TUESDAY **3** NOVEMBER

This morning we set out in the direction of Kilaguni Lodge. Large flocks of helmeted guinea fowl scratch the ground near the track, covering themselves in clouds of dust.

A group of zebras and fringe-eared oryxes drink at an almost dry water-hole. And we get our first look at the distinctively coloured wart hogs of Tsavo. Though naturally grey-brown in colour, like wart hogs elsewhere, they generally appear fiery-red here through rolling or wallowing (when it is muddy) in the red laterite soil.

Around the lodge the acacia trees are full of weaver bird nests, and there is much coming and going.

We drive on to Mtito Andei. On the way back we take the river circuit, where there are a number of baobab trees beside the road. Most of them are damaged by elephants, which tear off the bark during the dry season. In one

big baobab we see the head of a ground hornbill looking out of a large knot-hole. We assume that it is a nesting female — a fact that is confirmed shortly afterwards when two males, their bills packed with locusts and leaves, land on a branch in front of the hole. Soon they fly to the hole and throw their supplies inside. They return to the branch where they preen for a short while, then take off and land in the tall grass nearby.

We drive on to Mzima Springs. Here the water that originates in the Chyulu Hills bubbles out of the lava and feeds a small,

crystal-clear lake where there are some hippos and crocodiles, and many fishes, especially barbels. After lunch we explore some more of the park before arriving at Kilaguni Lodge at 5.00pm, where we stop for a drink at the bar. From the terrace there is a superb view of Kilimanjaro, the bush savannah, and the Chyulu Hills with Shaitani and its lava flow. At one of the artificial water-holes dug to attract the animals there are some zebras and waterbuck. A wart hog wallows in the mud and a flock of marabous flies in.

6.00pm The sun is about to set when a large herd of elephants appears. The animals rush forward into the water, some just drinking, while others spray water over their backs with much excited trumpeting. But they don't stay long. We had not expected anything to happen, and had left the cameras in the van. By the time Günter returns, the elephants are already leaving the water-holes. Günter is just saying that he will never get such a chance again when a second herd appears. They behave much like the first group, rushing into the water and then drinking thirstily, and bathing with a lot of noise. This time we capture the scene on film (31).

WEDNESDAY 4 NOVEMBER

7.00am We go straight to the baobab tree where we saw the ground hornbills yesterday. But we have to wait for two hours before the males arrive to feed the female. However, there is plenty to watch while we are waiting. A pair of broad-billed rollers are squabbling with a pair of red-billed hornbills and a pair of grey hornbills over another knot-hole in the baobab. Each pair of birds takes possession of the hole by turn, but none of them seem certain that they really want to stay there.

Eventually the two male ground hornbills arrive, feed the female, and leave. She follows them at 9.15am, but returns a quarter of an hour later and vanishes inside the hole.

Around noon we go to the Roaring Rocks near Kilaguni Lodge. Leaving the van we climb up the fifty-foot pile of boulders. There are two klipspringers at the top, but they run away when we arrive. Lizards of several species disappear into crevices.

We look down on Rhino Valley and the adjacent plain where we can see a small river bordered with douma palms. A herd of elephants heads across the plain.

SATURDAY 21 NOVEMBER

Today is a 'hornbill day'. First we visit the family that are nesting near Kilaguni Lodge, but nothing much is happening so we leave them and drive on to the other group in the baobab tree. On the way we stop to watch a pair of red-billed hornbills collecting mud from a puddle on the track.

They fly to a hole in a nearby tree, and plaster the mud around the hole. Later the female will enter the hole and she will complete the process of plastering from inside, using her droppings to shut the entrance: she will leave a gap about half an inch wide through which the male will pass food for the incubating female and later for the young as well, when they hatch.

We watch this activity for more than three hours. When the birds stop we drive on and spend the rest of the day with the ground hornbills at the baobab tree.

This species is the largest of the hornbills. The female is not confined to the nest-hole, as with other species, but she only leaves her eggs for short periods, and is fed by several birds belonging to the family group.

MONDAY 23 NOVEMBER

10.30am We have to go to the workshop at Park Headquarters to have a puncture repaired, and, while we are waiting, take the chance to photograph some weaver birds (32). A big yellow-barked acacia is festooned with nests, each of which has a male weaver clinging to the entrance, singing with head downwards and wings flapping, trying to attract a female. It is quite noisy, with about 100 male birds competing for the favours of the females. This is a time of feverish activity for the weaver birds, who need to compress nest-building, courtship, breeding, and rearing of their young into the short period when there is abundant green vegetation following the brief rains.

32

After lunch we return to the camp-site at Chyulu Gate, and at about 3.00pm meet two pairs of ostriches. Unlike all the other ostriches we have encountered, these ones do not run away from the van, so we stay with them and watch them feeding. On the other side of the track a lilac-breasted roller sits watching us from a bush (33). We had already met this beautifully coloured bird in the Masai Mara, but had not been able to photograph it.

Suddenly one of the male ostriches chases the other male, flapping its wings aggressively (34). But the pursuit is short-lived. We reckon that one of the females had joined the second pair, so her partner had to attack the other male in order to get her back.

7.00am We leave our camp-site at the Chyulu Gate, and we drive along the river circuit towards Mtito Andei. As we are passing a tree that has partly fallen over, we notice a yellow-billed hornbill sitting on it with food in its beak. We stop, and while we are wondering where the nest may be, the bird flies to the ground, hops under the tree trunk, then flies up and delivers the food to a hole on the underside of the trunk. When it flies away we take the chance to have a closer look at the site.

We already know something about the odd breeding behaviour of hornbills (it is mentioned on page 62), but it is exciting to see it with our own eyes. Having enclosed the female, the male bird has left an opening slightly more than half an inch wide, and about four inches long, through which we can just see the female. The young have not yet hatched.

We go back to the van and look for a good vantage point from which to photograph the male when it returns with more food. It appears quite soon with a locust in its bill, and lands on the trunk. After looking around it drops to the ground and then flies up to pass

34

the food morsel to its mate while still in flight (35). We stay there watching and photographing for more than three hours, marvelling at the diligence with which the male bird looks after its mate.

TUESDAY 1 DECEMBER

11.00am It is our last day in Tsavo National Park, and so we drive over to Kilaguni Lodge for lunch. From the terrace outside the bar we enjoy the panorama with Kilimanjaro in the distance. Many weaver birds and a few red-billed hornbills hop around on the guard-rail and the tables, looking for scraps left by tourists.

35

We hear a strange twittering noise, and get up to look over the rail. What we see are not birds but a party of ten dwarf mongooses running through the grass, the adults in front with the youngsters bringing up the rear.

While Günter hurries back to the van to get his camera, some other people on the terrace see the mongooses as well. One man cries out, 'Rats. Look at the rats!' In fact they bear little resemblance to rats, looking more like weasels — but perhaps the man had never seen a weasel before either.

The mongooses are very wary. Often one of the adults will interrupt its search for food,

stand up on its hind-legs, and survey the surroundings (36). Another climbs a pile of stones and keeps watch from there. All the time the animals are twittering, which is how they maintain contact when they cannot see one another.

One adult finds a big dung beetle and runs with it to a stone-pile, disappearing inside.

Two youngsters are scuffling and chasing each other when there is a sudden sharp whistling sound. All the mongooses dive into the nearest hole or hide among the stones. But it was only the sound of a chair being moved that had frightened one of them, and caused him to sound the alarm. Soon they are peering out of their hiding places, and then resume their search for food.

*2.30*pm We pay a last visit to the Roaring Rocks and then drive on to Chiemu Crater, an old volcano which gives the impression that its last eruption was only a few days ago.

The track goes up the lava flow, then circles the volcano before descending into Rhino Valley. A group of elephants is feeding among the bushes on the slope, and if they were not

moving one might almost mistake them for red laterite rocks.

Down in the valley we stop to look at another party of elephants with some calves. A young bull calf tries to impress us by advancing with a lot of snorting and ear-flapping. We laugh at his antics, but when one of the adults starts to follow the young bull's example, we decide to leave voluntarily.

5.30pm Nine lions cross in front of us. The four males have no manes, which is typical of Tsavo lions. They lie down in the bushes while the females stalk a kongoni. It is getting late and a thunderstorm is building up in the north.

6.15pm We return to Kila-guni Lodge, and then head back to our camp-site at the Chyulu Gate. Shortly after leaving the main road we spot a leopard standing on the branch of a dead tree beside the track (37). A shaft of light from the dying sun breaks through the clouds and touches this wonderful cat, its muscles tense in the expectation of a hunt. Without warning the leopard crouches, then jumps down from the tree and immediately sprints across the road only fifty yards in front of us, chasing a small animal into the bushes.

6.45pm We arrive at our camp-site at 7.00pm, just before the gate closes. It is dark by now, and we are not sure whether we had really seen the leopard, or if we had simply dreamed it. While I start to prepare dinner, Günter takes his camera and flash to photograph some nocturnal insects in the bushes. By chance he comes across two common genets. They stare at him for a few seconds, their eyes glowing in the torchlight (38), then vanish into the bushes.

The next day we return to Nairobi.

38

FOUR

MASAI MARA II

We spend a few days in Nairobi, sending off film for processing collecting more film, and buying food and other supplies for our second visit to the Masai Mara National Reserve.

TUESDAY 8 DECEMBER

The sun is finally shining again after several days of rain as we set out from Nairobi early in the morning. Crossing the plain at the bottom of the Rift Valley, we come across a kongoni calf lying beside the road. It has probably been killed by a car.

39

10.30am We stop and watch as a white-backed vulture glides down with its feet lowered like an aircraft undercarriage (39), to land by the carcass. It joins others of its kind, as well as a number of Ruppell's and lappet-faced vultures, and three golden jackals that are already there (40). As we watch, more and more vultures arrive, growling and screaming with wings spread as they advance to join the throng. Soon the birds are nearly standing on top of each other as they strive to plunge their heads inside the dead calf.

After an hour there is not much left and we leave, driving to Governor's Camp, and then to our camp-site near the Balloon House, where we immediately feel at home.

WEDNESDAY 9 DECEMBER
MASAI MARA 1981

We go to the marsh in the morning to look for the hyenas. From some distance away we can see many black and white dots covering the northern part of the marsh. They turn out to be European storks — more than 100 of them. As soon as the morning breeze develops the storks take wing, looking for the thermal air currents that will carry them high into the sky. They circle above us before disappearing over the riverine forest.

The hyenas have a den near a dead tree on the edge of the marsh, but we do not stay long as only one female and several juveniles are present.

We drive on and near Fig Tree Forest find the three lionesses — Diana and the two sisters — resting in the shade of a tree.

After lunch at the camp-site we drive out again and find the lionesses still in the same position. Even a shower of rain doesn't seem to wake them up.

Later we meet a family group of ground hornbills. One of the males catches a frog. The female approaches, makes a begging gesture, and takes it from him.

THURSDAY 10 DECEMBER

We go for a game drive in the afternoon and find a big herd of elephants grazing at the edge of Fig Tree Forest.

Many of the cows are accompanied by very young calves. One cow is followed closely by a young bull, who caresses her ears with his trunk while walking behind and beside her. He tries to mount her a couple of times, and the older bulls appear to tolerate this, so perhaps she is not yet in oestrus.

The elephants move away, so we drive to the marsh where a pair of crowned cranes are feeding. Just before sunset another pair of cranes fly in and land in the marsh beside the resident pair. The residents run towards the intruders, but they fail to frighten them away, and soon both pairs are feeding alongside one another. However, this feeding seems to be more ritual than reality, with the birds pecking the ground and symbolically feeding their partners. It is a 'displacement activity': a concentration on some commonplace activity that results when there is a conflict between the natural tendency either to fight or retreat.

On our way back to the camp-site we see an aardwolf for the first time.

6.25am We are back at the marsh before sunrise and the four crowned cranes are still where we left them yesterday. They seem to have spent the night on the ground, which is quite unusual for these birds that normally roost in tree-tops.

The birds are still feeding close together, but aggression is building up. Suddenly the resident pair approaches the intruders with wings flapping (41), then both pairs are in the air together (42), kicking out their legs at the opposing pair. The skirmish ends abruptly and they resume feeding. There are three more of these confrontations but after the last one the intruding pair takes off and flies away, accompanied by the trumpeting calls of the victors.

We drive to the other side of the marsh where some zebras are grazing. One mare has a tiny foal, and we watch them for a while.

In the afternoon we go to the murram pit water-hole at the airstrip where we meet the zoologist Jonathan Scott. He tells us about a lioness with four three- to four-week-old cubs hidden under a dead Euphorbia.

We follow Jonathan to the eastern edge of Rhino Ridge, where the ground is covered with stones and boulders, and we can only drive to the Euphorbia with difficulty. The tree is lying on the ground and the lioness has hidden her cubs — which are about the size of domestic cats — in the crown. They look at us

42

with curiosity and then continue clambering over their mother, who is lying inside.

In a little while the lioness comes out and stalks a passing topi. The tiny cubs, who are barely able to walk, climb and stumble over the branches and then come to the entrance of their 'cave' to watch their mother (43). Eventually the lioness returns, disturbed by the approach of another vehicle. We depart soon afterwards and drive along the ridge, then back to our camp-site.

SATURDAY 12 DECEMBER

Today we discover the nest of the four ground hornbills which we had seen at the marsh three days ago. The hole itself is in the broken branch of the big fig tree that gave Fig Tree Forest its name.

We park nearby and wait for the birds, which generally prefer to walk than fly. We had seen two of them, an adult male and a juvenile, on the way. The male had a snake in his bill. But before they arrive the second male flies to the tree with a beakload of food, a mixture of frogs and beetles.

He lands above the hole and throws the food inside, then flies away to join the other two, who are still walking towards the tree. Soon the female emerges and flies to join them as well. Ten minutes later she returns to the hole with a snake (most probably the one the male was carrying) and starts to feed. We can hear weak begging calls from the young bird, which is already about two months old.

SUNDAY 13 DECEMBER

6.30am We set off before sunrise for the murram pit water-hole at the airstrip, where we find nearly all the members of the airstrip lion pride waiting for the first warming rays of sun. We count three adult females and six juveniles. The younger animals scuffle among themselves for a while, and then the three adults and one juvenile leave for Fig Tree Forest.

Two of the adults try to hunt some zebras, but the stallions are on the alert and have no difficulty in protecting their females.

So the four lions head for the shade beneath a tree, next to the big fig tree in which the hornbills are nesting, where they settle down. Soon the rest of the lions have joined them, and all nine are sprawled out in the patch of shade (44,45).

45

We notice flashes of white at the edge of the forest: they turn out to be the undersides of some vultures' wings. Through binoculars we can see that a zebra is chasing the vultures and keeping them away from something that is hidden in the tall grass.

Driving closer, we meet a pair of black-backed jackals sneaking through the grass, trying to approach a dead newborn zebra foal, which the mare is defending vigorously. The other zebras are grazing not far away.

46

Before long the mare gives up and rejoins the rest of the herd, but not without neighing in a rather mournful way. As soon as the zebra leaves the scene, vultures arrive from all around. But the jackals are there first and keep the vultures away while they tear off some pieces of meat for themselves (46). Then they, too, retire, leaving the carcass to the assembled vultures.

Within seconds the voracious beaks have opened up the body. From time to time we glimpse a bloody head, raised for a moment before plunging back into the melee.

None of them has reckoned on the zebra mare returning, which she now does without warning. The vultures scatter in all directions, and then the zebra leaves again. She has barely turned her back before the vultures are all over the carcass. But now it is the turn of the jackals to come back for more, and once again the vultures are driven off. Nevertheless, the birds are very persistent, and there are always one or two beaks darting in to snatch a morsel.

At this point the zebra returns for the second time, and chases the jackals away. But on this occasion she pursues them until they vanish into the forest.

9.00am We go back to the resting lions, but all is quiet. Only the tips of their tails are moving.

2.00pm In the distance a lone zebra is grazing. When the lions become aware of its presence, two of them get to their feet and start stalking it. But the zebra is lucky and is able to escape. Now the plains are empty, and we and the lions bide our time.

6.00pm Two zebra herds approach from Fig Tree Forest. They have been grazing on the other side of the forest and now spread out onto the plain for the night. They feel more secure here than in the woodland, or between the riverine forest and Fig Tree Forest. Each herd of zebras has a tiny foal. Now the lions are fully awake, and stare at the zebras with every muscle tense.

Two lionesses get up and stalk one herd, while the third adult uses our van as cover to stalk the other group. We are well placed to watch her at close range, and can see her taut muscles and how she peers through the tall grass without being spotted by her prey.

By now the other two lionesses have reached the herd. One of them stands up and frightens the zebras, which take off towards the second lioness. She catches the foal.

The other lions promptly rush up but the successful female will only allow one juvenile to join her. As both start to eat, the other two females walk back to the water-hole.

THURSDAY 17 DECEMBER

After three afternoons of rain we have to stay on the murram-surfaced road when we go out, or else we may get stuck.

We come to two pools at the culvert under the road, not far outside the camp. A saddle-billed stork is fishing in one of them, and catches a frog. But then the stork is attacked by a black kite that dives down from above. The frog manages to get free and leaps back into the water.

Another thunderstorm moves in from the east and we turn back.

FRIDAY 18 DECEMBER

Today it is raining and we stay at our camp-site near the Balloon House. We are just about to have lunch when a huge bull elephant walks out of the forest. He passes within about five yards of us, but disregards us completely (see photograph on page 8).

We follow as he walks on towards the staff houses. Women take their children out of his way as he walks straight through the laundry, bending his head to avoid the clothesline. Now we can guess where he is heading — and sure enough, he walks straight to the back of the kitchen and empties the waste buckets. We find out later that his name is 'Wendy', and that he is a regular visitor to the camp.

WEDNESDAY 23 DECEMBER

We visit the hyena den and meet Eve again for the first time since we were last in the Mara. Her two cubs have grown considerably. Their heads are now a creamy colour and the spots on their bodies are quite distinct. Only their legs are still black.

We spend the rest of the morning watching some ostriches (four males and four females). They are in breeding plumage, with pink legs and necks in splendid contrast to their black and white feathers.

47

MASAI MARA 1981

THURSDAY 24 DECEMBER

7.00am We return to the hyena den. From the slope we hear hyenas calling and we drive close. Two young males are trying to approach a female that is probably in oestrus. She growls and screams at them each time they come near. Then more males join in. It can be very difficult to tell a male from a female as the female's external genitalia are unusually well developed. Sometimes one can only judge from observing typical behaviour and situations.

The males gather in a big circle round the female, who sits on her backside and screams loudly at them. Then the whole pack moves off into the riverine forest.

On our way back to the camp-site we pass a group of banded mongooses sunning themselves on a termite mound (47). They dive into their numerous holes when we stop, but after a few minutes their heads appear. They creep out cautiously, but at the slightest sound they dive out of sight again.

After lunch we look for a Christmas tree, choosing a big branch that has been broken off in a storm. It is covered with yellow, orange, and red fruits, and looks pretty when planted in an empty tin and decorated with small candles.

As darkness falls we sit and listen to the voices of the African night. It is my first Christmas without snow — but somehow I feel at home. We go to the main camp for dinner, and enjoy a happy, convivial evening with turkey and Christmas pudding.

After spending the morning with the hyenas we return to the camp-site for lunch. I go to the bar to get some soft drinks, while Günter prepares the meal. On my way back I nearly bump into Wendy, the elephant bull, who is on his way back too. I keep behind him.

Günter sees us coming and retreats inside the van. I wait behind a tree as Wendy heads straight for the fig tree beside our van. He adores the ripe figs and picks one after another. But then he smells our lunch, and starts to fumble with his trunk at the raised roof of the van. Günter pulls the roof down, but Wendy lifts it up again. Günter pulls it down once more, and this time Wendy tries to raise it with his tusks. Fortunately, he abandons this before any damage is done. I am shaking with laughter, but Günter is not so happy.

*10.30*am Some vultures are circling above Rhino Ridge, so we drive there to investigate. A male black-backed jackal is carrying the head of a young Thomson's gazelle towards a patch of grass near a pool (48). A female follows. The male hides his prey in the grass, then both lie down. Their bellies are round and full. Two other jackals are walking around nearby, and our two get up and go towards them.

Then the female comes back, retrieves the Tommy's head, and runs with it to a termite mound where she starts to eat again. There will not be much left for the vultures by the time she has finished.

In the evening we join the Governor's Camp New Year's Eve party. Some Masai have come from a nearby village and dance around the fire. There is a delicious dinner of roasted meat, and then we settle down by the fire. The drivers have put on costumes, and they too are dancing and singing. We cannot understand the words, but their gaiety is infectious.

48

81

SATURDAY 2 JANUARY

This morning we take a short game drive outside the reserve, and then return to the camp-site for lunch.

Today it is Günter's turn to get the soft drinks, while I make lunch in the van. Looking up by chance I see Wendy coming towards me from the Balloon House. He is about thirty yards away, and I just have time to close the front window on my side and get back inside. But the front window on the other side is still open — and Wendy, it appears, has nothing better to do than to poke his trunk inside.

The front part of the van is separated from the rear (where I am) by a wooden partition with a door. Looking through my window I can see the big elephant close enough to touch. Then I see his trunk come out of the van, holding Günter's sweater. He throws it around for a while and tries to eat it, but then drops it and comes back to the window.

This time he has my microphone and headphones, which are wrapped in a plastic bag. He opens the bag with a tusk and takes out the headphones. These he carefully takes to bits, then picks up the microphone.

At this point I summon my courage and leave the van, for I have to try to save the cameras, which are also lying in the front.

Only the van is between me and Wendy as I slowly open the door and remove the cameras. Wendy looks at me with his tiny eyes. He seems a little surprised, but then just turns away and walks off.

I go round to the other side and pick up my microphone and headphones. Fortunately, they are still in working order. Günter's sweater is rather muddy, however.

In the afternoon we drive outside the reserve along Fig Tree Ridge. We decide to spend the night there near Eagle-Owl Grove.

7.00pm While I make dinner Günter explores our surroundings. Only a few yards away he finds some little bee-eaters that have chosen to spend the night sleeping in a bush. When it is completely dark he returns with his flash and photographs them nestling against each other on a small branch (49).

Nightjars call and the moon is nearly full.

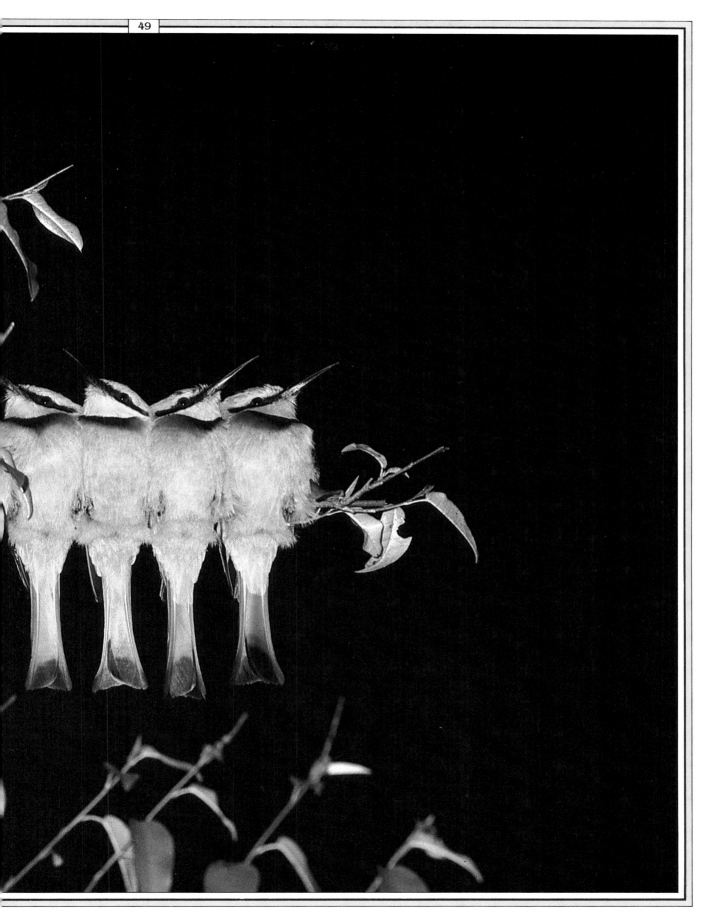

MONDAY 4 JANUARY

7.00am We drive to Rhino Ridge, and as we are scanning the plain through binoculars, we notice some hyenas chasing a wildebeest calf. We drive down the slope as fast as we can, but miss the kill by a few seconds.

The hyenas seem very hungry and make a lot of noise. More and more arrive from every direction, including about twenty members of another clan. But the owners of the territory drive them off before they can get near the carcass. Within about fifteen minutes nothing is left but the head and tail, and some juveniles are even fighting about these left-overs. About sixty hyenas have tried to get a piece of meat, but only twenty managed to share the meal.

TUESDAY 5 JANUARY

We are back in Paradise Plain before sunrise and locate the lions easily enough from the circling vultures.

A male and a female lion each have a wildebeest carcass, while another female sprawls nearby, her belly distended with food. Many vultures have gathered round the lioness with the carcass. But although she is not hungry she cannot bear them getting too close, and is constantly leaping up and scattering them. Once she jumps into the air, swiping at the big birds with her paws.

WEDNESDAY 6 JANUARY

6.30am We arrive at the fallen Euphorbia on Rhino Ridge, where we had seen a lioness with her cubs on 11 December. She is still there, lying in front of the tree with her cubs beside her. They are hungry, and whimper and cry until she turns on her back and allows them to suckle (50). Eventually they fall asleep while feeding.

The other members of the pride are lying among the rocks, and not far away a female rhino is grazing. For the juvenile lions she becomes a new playmate, with whom they

85

can practise stalking. The rhino takes no notice of them at all.

The lioness moves with her cubs to the shade of the Euphorbia. The cubs are fully awake now and are exploring their mother. They enjoy climbing over her, but their favourite pastime is trying to catch the moving tip of her tail.

Suddenly the lioness stands up, looks down the hill briefly, then runs off leaving the cubs who retreat under the tree. We cannot see where she goes, but she is back within five minutes, carrying a young impala (51). She growls softly, calling her cubs. They approach with curiosity, but when they come a bit closer she pushes them away with her paw.

Some of the juvenile lions have followed the lioness, and now they also come closer. But she shows her teeth and growls loudly (52), which is enough to discourage them. Then

she lies down with the impala between her legs and starts to eat. The cubs play with the tip of her tail, but again she pushes them away if they come too near her prey.

The lioness finishes eating the impala on her own, whereupon she stands up and obviously wants to go. She tries to make her cubs follow, but they are reluctant to leave, and run around her playfully. She then picks one of them up and is about to carry it away, when another cub bites the tip of her tail. The long-suffering mother lets the first cub drop and turns her head to growl with impatience at the one behind (53).

11.00am We drive on to Paradise Plain where in the Little Wood we discover four lionesses and four cubs about six weeks old (roughly the same age as those on Rhino Ridge). But as they are hiding in the undergrowth we can hardly see them.

12.00am A mass of vultures attracts our attention, so we drive about 200 yards where we discover a dead male Thomson's gazelle (54 overleaf). The lionesses have also seen the vultures, and a few minutes later one of them has arrived, seizes the carcass, and drags it to a patch of grass.

Two more lionesses follow her and approach very cautiously. They both lie down when a dull growling warns them not to come any closer. After a few moments they start to edge forward again, but there is a certain distance beyond which they dare not go. The feeding lioness clearly does not intend to share her meal, and, in fact, she eventually finishes off the gazelle on her own.

53

FRIDAY **8** JANUARY

MONDAY **11** JANUARY

7.30am Mist hangs over the plains, and on the slopes of Paradise Hill a group of topis stands forlornly (55). The sun appears above the horizon like a fiery ball, casting its still faint light across the scene.

Down on the plain itself the mist has dissolved and the Paradise lions are lying in the grass, which is wet with dew. As the sun rises the lions' manes turn gold and the grass takes on a deep blue-green colour, with a few scattered golden stems. Two lionesses lying apart from the males get up first and walk to the rocks of Paradise Hill. The males set off after them.

In the afternoon we stay with the two lion sisters, near the camp-site. Twice they attempt to hunt — first a wart hog, then a zebra but they are unsuccessful.

7.30am In the morning we can find nothing but lions — thirty-five of them in three hours of driving.

2.30pm After lunch we return to Paradise Plain and find some grazing zebras. A young foal is sleeping beside the track, but does not wake until we have already been there for a while. It looks at us sleepily, and when we drive slowly on it seems to think that our van is its mother, for it follows us. We stop again and the foal whinnies. The other zebras, especially the foal's mother, are upset. The mother calls and calls, but the youngster stays with us.

Finally the foal leaves. It returns to the herd, where the mare suckles it (56).

We continue driving and on top of Rhino Ridge we encounter five lionesses. At sunset they get to their feet and walk down the slope towards some wildebeest. When they are about 100 yards away they lie down and wait for darkness to fall.

55

MONDAY 18 JANUARY

This morning we watch a cheetah stalking a group of Tommies on Paradise Plain, but they realize the danger thanks to a topi which snorts an alarm. While the cheetah waits in the

58

shade, we observe a tawny eagle eating a dwarf mongoose in a dead tree (57). When he has nearly finished he is attacked and driven off by a hooded vulture. But the vulture in turn is mobbed by a black kite (58), though he manages to stand his ground.

5.30pm *The cheetah gets up and walks, at first without any apparent aim. But then she spots a male Tommy, and starts to trot. At about 100 yards she hides behind a termite mound. Ten minutes pass and when the Tommy's back is turned the cheetah breaks cover and runs towards him. Then she sprints (59 overleaf), and is only thirty yards away when he spots her. They pass us at a colossal speed. The cheetah cannot get quite close enough, however, and after about 300 yards she gives up and lies down panting on a termite mound.*

TUESDAY **19** JANUARY

We set out early for Paradise Plain, but the lions are not active, so after a short while we return to Governor's Camp.

9.30am It is breakfast time and the tables are set up out of doors. Suddenly Wendy arrives. At first he goes behind the bar where he leans against a tree, trying to shake some fruit to the ground. But he isn't very successful and decides to join the tourists at breakfast.

He walks straight to the nearest table where two Japanese girls, who appear to be fashion models, are being photographed. The photographer cannot persuade them to stay in their seats so Wendy has the table to himself (60). First he tries some papaya, then a piece of melon, and then some bread. But even Wendy cannot eat his breakfast undisturbed, for the waiters start to throw things at him, even chairs, to get him to move away.

It is hard to enjoy a meal when chairs are being thrown at you, and so finally, looking rather discontented, Wendy leaves the table and goes off to the kitchen.

3.00pm This afternoon we drive out to Rhino Ridge once again, where we find two pairs of lions, each of which has settled under trees about 200 yards apart.

Both pairs are mating, but we are interested to see that the temper of love differs among lions as it does among humans. One lioness, for example, is always trying to run away from her male. He has to chase her, and when he catches her he has to slap her with his paw until finally she is willing to let him mount (61). But at the end he has to jump off quickly as she tries to bite him.

The other pair are much calmer and the male mounts much more often, about every five minutes.

The sun is about to set when Günter notices that one of the lionesses is staring into the distance instead of making love. Looking around he sees two men walking along with a jerry-can, about only 200 yards from the lions. So we drive over to the men, who tell us that they have run out of petrol and are walking to Governor's Camp to get some more. We drive them back to their car on the other side of the ridge, and give them some of our petrol so that they can return to their camp outside the reserve.

FRIDAY **22** JANUARY

Today is our last day in the Masai Mara, so we make a round trip visiting all the places that we have been to in the last few weeks. We spend the night outside the reserve, near some flowering acacias. The sweet smell hangs in the air. And once again at nightfall we listen to the singing of cicadas and grasshoppers and distant calls of hyenas. Tomorrow we shall head back to Nairobi.

MOUNT KENYA

Mount Kenya is an old shield volcano, formed at the same time as the Great Rift Valley some twenty to thirty million years ago. It rises from farmland and plains about seventy-five miles north-east of Nairobi and is some 250 miles in circumference. The national park itself, which was established in 1949, covers some 276 square miles and includes all of the mountain above the 10,500-foot contour, plus two lower ridges at Sirimon and Naro Moru. At lower levels Mount Kenya is clothed in forest, where there are a number of interesting mammals, such as leopard, bongo antelope, and black and white colobus monkey. Elephants are regularly seen up to 13,000 feet.

As altitude increases the forest is replaced by dense bamboo and a small zone of giant heaths (growing to twenty-five feet), followed by Hypericum scrub (St John's wort family) where there are two endemic animals — the giant Mount Kenya mole rat, and the Mount Kenya mole shrew. The Hypericum zone grades into open alpine moorland with giant lobelias (*Lobelia keniensis*), groundsels (*Senecio brassica*) and thistles. Higher still are about thirty lakes and tarns and a dozen little glaciers dominated by three snow-capped peaks — Batian (17,058 feet), Nelion (17,022 feet), and Lenana (16,355 feet). All three peaks are actually volcanic plugs exposed by erosion of the original crater rim.

The Kikuyu people revere *Kilinyaa* (The White Mountain), as they call it, which they consider to be the home of their god *Mwene-Nyaga* (Possessor of Mystery). The whole area of the park is open to visitors, but the southern part is deliberately kept free of trails and other development. The peaks are popular with mountaineers, though they should be treated with respect.

Tree groundsels near Hut Tarn, with Batian and Nelion, Mount Kenya's highest peaks, in the background.

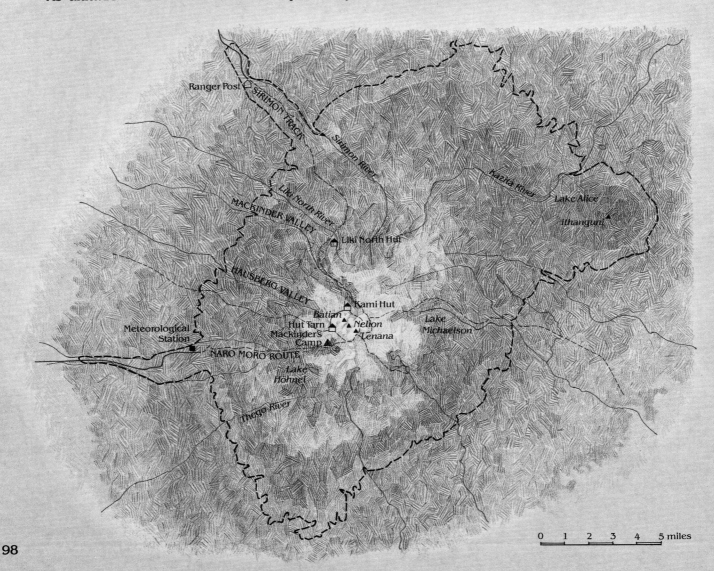

62

MONDAY 1 FEBRUARY

We leave Nairobi in the morning, driving northwards through Kenya's Central Province which stretches between the Aberdares and Mount Kenya. This is Kikuyu country. The Kikuyus are farmers and the landscape is largely cultivated fields.

We reach Naro Moru River Lodge in the afternoon. This lodge, on the mountain's lower slopes, is the starting point for visits to Mount Kenya using the Naro Moru route. Most of the climbers take this route as it provides the quickest access to the peaks. But since we would prefer to avoid other people, we decide to take the Sirimon track instead, then walk the circuit around the peaks before returning via the Naro Moru route.

We camp at a wonderful site beside the riverine forest, and quite near the lodge.

WEDNESDAY 3 FEBRUARY

After a day spent in the vicinity of the camp-site we head north again, and cross the Equator just before reaching Nanyuki. About nine miles past Nanyuki we turn off to the right. This is the Sirimon track, which leads up the northern flank of Mount Kenya.

The slopes of Mount Kenya are cultivated up to the boundaries of the national park, and although we drive through forest, it is not natural forest but plantations of cedar and pine. Not until we reach the immediate vicinity of the gate, located in a clearing at about 6,500 feet, do we encounter the original forest. Here trees such as Hagenia and Podocarpus still predominate.

In the distance we can see a gorge, carved through the rocks by the Sirimon, one of the many rivers that flow down from the mountain. It would have been possible to drive up to 10,500 feet, using a vehicle having four-wheel-drive, but ours does not so we have to leave it in the care of the rangers. Before turning in we pack our rucksacks so that we can make an early start in the morning.

THURSDAY 4 FEBRUARY

We leave the ranger post and enter the forest soon after sunrise. The track runs more or less parallel to the river, which is on our left, deep down in the gorge.

The trees are massive, reaching far up above us. The dense undergrowth consists mainly of bamboo. Here and there is an elephant or buffalo trail. Parrots call loudly in the tree tops. The forest thins out as we climb higher. In a clearing we meet some zebras, and a party of baboons disappears noisily into the bushes, the leading males barking in alarm. We are happy not to meet any buffalo.

We finally leave the forest at about 10,000 feet and enter the area of vast heaths and Hypericum. The former, which grow to about two feet in Europe, are here large flowering bushes. But this zone soon ends and we are walking across grassland.

At 10,500 feet the track ends at a small stream. We choose a small plateau, with a wonderful view of the plains below, as a site for our tent.

FRIDAY 5 FEBRUARY

The temperature dropped to freezing during the night, so in the morning we wait for the sun's early warmth before getting up.

The track now twists through clumps of grass and heather. Soon we see the masses of groundsels and young giant lobelias, and we realize that we have reached the moorlands. We stop to watch a male scarlet-tufted malachite sunbird feeding on the hidden flowers of the giant lobelias (62). These birds do not occur much below 13,000 feet and are specialized feeders on the lobelias. Rainwater has collected at the base of the lobelia leaves (63 overleaf), and mosquitoes seem to use these little reservoirs to breed, as we see a number of larvae. We reach a small valley at about 13,000 feet through which a stream is flowing. There has been a fire and burnt tree groundsels (Senecio keniodendron) cover the slopes. They must have formed a considerable forest at one time. There is elephant dung everywhere (the animals come here at certain times of the year to feed on the groundsels).

Walking uphill again we reach a ridge and see the snowy peaks of Mount Kenya rise before us. Only the valley of the Liki North, a small river some 600 feet below, now separates us from the peaks of Batian and Nelion. But we don't want to go much farther today,

101

so we head down the rocky slopes of the valley to the Liki North mountaineer's hut.

Crossing the river we walk upstream to the hut, which sits among lichen-covered rocks at the foot of the slope. Rock hyraxes are sunning themselves in cracks and crevices, and we can see their tracks leading to where they feed near the river.

There is a cave on the opposite slope, where we observe three eland in the late afternoon. We presume they have climbed up to this altitude to lick the mineral salts from the rocks.

Lifting up our rucksacks we say goodbye to the Liki North valley, and follow the red and white posts that mark the track which snakes up the slope. At the top of the ridge we look down on Mackinder valley on the other side.

We carry on just below the ridge until we reach Kami Hut at 14,500 feet. Next we climb the scree slopes of Hausburg Col, a branch of the Nelion ridge and a little peak in its own right. Arriving at a small pass we are disappointed to find that the peaks of Mount Kenya are hidden in cloud.

Finally we reach Hut Tarn (named after a

64

MOUNT KENYA 1982

SATURDAY **6** FEBRUARY

In the morning the grass is covered with hoar-frost. The river is frozen in some places and even the water trapped in the giant lobelias has a thin layer of ice. The ice does not melt until the sun rises. A rock hyrax studies Günter intently as he photographs it (64). He and his companions are feeling the cold and they sit crowded together on the rocks, some young ones on their mothers' backs (65), waiting for the sun to warm them up. We, too, enjoy the sun's warmth.

nearby mountaineer's hut) where we plan to spend the night. The clouds lift by late afternoon, and we can see Batian and Nelion reflected in the tarn's deep green water, with young tree groundsels and lobelias around the shore (see photograph on page 99).

After climbing another ridge and crossing the moorland, we reach the meteorological station. From here a land-cruiser belonging to the Naro Moru River Lodge takes us down.

Our first safari to Africa comes to an end. We return to Europe to have a break and to check the results of our photography. We plan to return in May, after the rainy season.

65

SIX

THE LAKES

The floor of East Africa's Great Rift Valley is marked by a series of lakes that are mostly rather bitter from sodium bicarbonate of volcanic origin. A few, however, contain fresh water, probably because they have underwater outlets through which the mineral salts can wash away.

Lake Naivasha is a freshwater lake surrounded by agricultural land, about fifty miles from Nairobi, and famous for its water birds and water lilies. Unfortunately, the latter have been destroyed by coypus that probably escaped from a fur farm. The ecological balance has also been disturbed by introduced fish species, but most water-loving birds still remain.

Lake Nakuru is a shallow, very alkaline soda lake just to the south of Nakuru Town. World-famous for birds, especially flamingos, it was declared a national park in 1967. There was a disaster in 1974 when the blue-green algae, on which the lesser flamingos depend, disappeared — and along with it the flamingos. Pollution from the town was probably a major factor, but a purification plant has now been built and the flamingos are starting to return.

Lake Bogoria (formerly Hannington) is another alkaline lake in the Great Rift Valley, about forty miles from Nakuru, and is noted for large numbers of greater and lesser flamingos. Another speciality is the greater kudu (spiral-horned antelope), which can be seen (with luck) on the eastern shores.

Euphorbias silhouetted against the dawn sky on the freshwater Lake Naivasha.

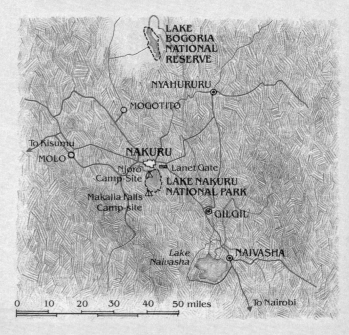

FRIDAY 14 MAY

We set out for Lake Naivasha, taking the new road along the escarpment. Bunches of rhubarb, pears, and carrots are laid out on the roadside, waiting for customers.

In due course we reach the observation point where the Great Rift Valley spreads out below us and the road descends towards the town of Naivasha.

We pass the town and turn off left onto the lake road. Still some distance from the lake, we are driving through farmland. There are many Euphorbias and Opuntia cactuses. Passing two small gorges, where hyraxes are sunning on the rocks, we begin to make out the shoreline of the lake from the patches of papyrus in the distance.

We arrive at Mennell's Farm, bordering the lake, where the owner — an Englishman — has opened a camp-site on his land. We look for a place for our van under tall yellow-barked acacias (fever trees) where fish eagles build their nests.

Eager to explore our surroundings, we go for a walk but find that we cannot get to the lake shore because of a large stretch of papyrus. So we climb a rocky hill where sunbirds are singing among Euphorbias and various aloes. From the top of the hill we enjoy a wonderful view of the lake.

SATURDAY 15 MAY

6.00am Woken by the calling of fish eagles we scale the rocky hill that we climbed yesterday, reaching the top before the sun. The red and gold light pouring from the eastern sky makes the Euphorbias appear to be on fire. Then the sun itself rises above the horizon. Sunbirds sing and eagles call.

7.30am After breakfast we explore the farm area. There are many tunnels in the papyrus, where hippos have come ashore during the night to feed. A small snake (Hemirhagerrhis nototaenia) lies curled at the top of a papyrus stem, waiting for the sun to reach it (66). Where the papyrus is not too thick some jacanas pick their way across floating vegetation as they search for food.

SUNDAY 16 MAY

A morning mist hangs over the lake after a very cold night. We walk along the lake shore and on to the neighbouring farm where the papyrus has not yet taken hold, and where we can see open water. Dead trees poke their branches out of the water, and on one of these sits an African darter, its wings spread out to dry in the sun (67).

7.10am The mist dissolves as the sun rises. The fish eagles are still calling and soon one flies towards us. It lands on another dead tree, and calls again (68). We notice for the first time how it throws its head back as it nears the end of its series of calls (it also does this even in flight).

9.00am The eagle remains on the tree for more than half an hour, then starts to preen.

9.20am We leave the eagle and approach a goliath heron which is striding through the water near the shore. But it catches only tiny fishes, and we wait in vain for it to catch a bigger one.
We have also been unlucky in our search for the famous water lilies of Lake Naivasha. We go over to some fishermen who are coming ashore and ask them where the water lilies are. They tell us that coypus, brought to Kenya by the white man, have eaten the lilies. Now all of them are gone.

MONDAY 17 MAY

This morning we leave Lake Naivasha to drive to Lake Nakuru. Passing through Naivasha Town we drive on to the bottom of the Great Rift Valley, and on to Gilgil.
Some miles after Gilgil we stop to look down on Lake Elmentaita, the smallest soda lake in the Rift Valley. It lies in a farming area owned by Lord Delamere. In the distance we can see a lot of greater flamingos, which breed on small islands in the lake.

2.30pm We enter Lake Nakuru National Park at the northern end, via the Lanet Gate. The track leads down a hill to the lake, which is bordered here by acacia forest. Large groups of waterbuck are on the grassy plains (Lake Nakuru has the largest waterbuck population in Kenya).
We follow the road along the eastern shore where it runs fairly close to the lake. An escarpment rises on our left, which seems almost covered with tree-like Euphorbias. The track takes us through an almost pure Euphorbia forest. We are driving quite fast now because of the dark clouds building up behind the escarpment on the other side of the lake, so we don't see many of the water birds, apart from a few herons, ducks, and some lesser flamingos. Sometimes white pelicans cross the lake in a long line, flying very close to the water.

As we reach the southern end of the lake it starts to rain. The road becomes more slippery and we have some difficulty negotiating the last few miles to Makalia Falls camp-site.

TUESDAY 18 MAY

In the morning we decide to set out on foot to follow the river, walking in the steep gorge of the river to avoid being surprised by buffalos.
Here and there we pass steep clay cliffs at bends in the river. These are ideal sites for kingfishers and bee-eaters to make their nest holes. A paradise flycatcher has begun to build a nest in the branches of a tree overhanging the river.
We walk on, passing tracks made by buffalos down the banks on both sides. Then we find another paradise flycatcher. This one, too, has built its nest in an overhanging branch. It seems a good site for photography so we return to the van to collect a hide and some flash equipment. By the time we get back the birds have changed over and the female is sitting in the nest. Carefully we set up the hide, camera, and flash units. It is now 9.00am, and we sit down to wait.

111

9.20am The male bird arrives and announces his presence with a series of calls. The female leaves the nest and the male takes over (69).

10.00am When we get back to our camp-site we hear a pair of Verreaux's eagles calling from the direction of the escarpment. Guided by their calls, we locate the birds in a Euphorbia growing on the cliff. We climb up the escarpment and approach them slowly. The eagles ignore us and we are able to get within about twenty yards of them. They have apparently just started nest-building, and the larger female is standing on a loose heap of twigs.

Within minutes they take to the air, but after a short while one of them comes back with a twig in its beak and lands on the Euphorbia. The partner arrives soon afterwards with more nesting material. For about an hour we watch the eagles bringing back twigs, sometimes in their beaks (70), sometimes carrying them in their claws. Then they start to circle, moving upwards on the thermals, and we eventually lose sight of them.

In the early afternoon we set out in the van for the Njoro camp-site, which is situated by the edge of the lake. The tracks are still very slippery because of yesterday's rain, and for much of the way we have to drive across country.

The only mammals that we see are a group of baboons, some impalas and waterbuck.

The track approaches the lake shore, but there are only a few flamingos, yellow-billed storks, and marabous by the water's edge. Finally we enter a large fever acacia forest and arrive at the camp-site on the Njoro River. A

little farther on the track forks and one branch leads to the river mouth.

Here the lake is bordered with dead trees, but there are living trees as well, which are filled with nesting cormorants. Courtship displays and nest-building are still going on. Along the shore are some lesser flamingos and pelicans. The flamingos rest and preen while the pelicans go out fishing in small groups (71 overleaf).

THURSDAY 20 MAY

We leave the camp-site in the early morning and drive via Njoro Gate into Nakuru Town, for we need to buy some fresh food. Shopping takes up the whole morning, after which we leave the town and drive along the foot of Mengai Crater towards Lake Bogoria.

As we get nearer to the lake we see many lava boulders on the ground. Passing through Loboi Gate we soon see the edge of the lake ahead of us, marked by a line of thousands of lesser flamingos. They create a narrow band of pinkish-white that hugs the whole lake shore. At least a third of the birds are juveniles not yet in adult plumage and so are more white than pink.

We follow the road along the western side, where a small ridge rises from the lake. On the eastern side is the escarpment, above which we can now see a black wall of clouds. A strong breeze blows up and caps the waves in the lake with white crowns.

3.20pm We reach the camp-site in the midst of some acacia trees. A white mist billows from the hot springs nearby. The acacias are full of weaver bird nests. A large flock of flamingos has gathered in a bay where they are well protected from the wind and waves (72). In the light of the dying sun they seem to be even more pink than before. Then the rain comes; later in the evening the sky clears and we can see the stars.

FRIDAY 21 MAY

In the morning the sun is shining. We are having breakfast when a cheetah approaches from the lake, where it may have been hoping to find an easy kill. As soon as it sees us it runs across the road and up the ridge.

The weaver birds are very active today, building nests. Most of them are golden-backed weavers. The males are yellow with black heads and red eyes. The olive-brown females wander about among the trees, and when one gets near a nest the male starts to display, hanging head down at the entrance hole (73), or from a nearby twig.

If a female accepts a mate she flies away and returns with a piece of grass to begin lining the interior of the nest. Sometimes a male will start to build a second nest as soon as he has found a female for the first one.

Between the trees and the bushes some cardinal queleas are building their nests in long grass (74). The nests are very well hidden.

In the afternoon there is another thunderstorm. It only rains for half an hour, but for us it is welcome refreshment after a hot day.

SUNDAY 23 MAY

A pair of d'Arnaud's barbets claim the acacia forest as their territory, and announce the fact with a loud duet. I tape their concert and play it back to them. This causes them to come and look for the intruders. Finding nothing they start to call again loudly, as if to drive away their unseen rivals. While the birds are calling the female's tail stands up and swings from side to side (75).

Our trick with the tape recorder works once more, but then finally the barbets realize that there are no intruders, and they do not respond further.

MONDAY 24 MAY

Again we spend the morning watching the weaver birds displaying and nest-building. At about noon we leave the camp-site and drive to where the track crosses a dried-up river bed. We stop the van in order to explore the surrounding area. Close to where we park we find a pair of yellow-winged bats hanging in a tree. They briefly take to the air and then settle again in another tree. They call to each other during the flight and land side by side. Then they embrace and copulate several times (76). Finally they fly off again and we lose sight of them.

We drive on around the southern end of the lake towards another camp-site. Here the track runs very close to the lake, and we disturb a flock of flamingoes which takes to the air like a pink cloud as we pass by.

The camp-site is beside a stream among some fig trees. We wonder why many of the trees are leafless, but soon the reason becomes apparent. The leaves have been gobbled up by thousands of hungry caterpillars. However, the caterpillars have their predators, too — small, iridescent green bugs — which leave the sucked-out caterpillar skins hanging on the tree trunks.

A party of baboons passes by, followed by several Sykes' monkeys. Frogs begin calling at sunset, and some bats hunt for insects that are attracted by the light of our torch.

TUESDAY 25 MAY

For a while we watch the flamingos feeding. They swing their heads from side to side through the water, with beaks upside down and pointing backwards, as they sift out algae from the muddy water.

Then we drive back to the hot springs. We see some dik-diks, but they remain half-hidden in the bushes beside the track. Two female kudus suddenly bolt across in front of the van.

We turn right before we reach the river bed and select an acacia tree as our camp-site. It is very hot. By a bend in the river we find the nest hole of a grey-headed kingfisher. Flocks of red-billed queleas land in the bushes by the river to bathe or take a drink. It seems to be a popular bathing place, and pin-tailed and straw-tailed wydahs and various finches and doves come and go.

In our acacia a pair of superb starlings are lining their nest. Tirelessly they keep arriving with their beaks full of flamingo feathers.

At about 3.00pm dark clouds above the escarpment tell us that a thunderstorm is coming our way. A stiff breeze ruffles the lake, then a solid wall of rain moves steadily forward, envelops us, and passes on. That night the stars glitter in a clear sky.

FRIDAY 28 MAY

This morning there is a wind from the east which blows clouds of steam from the hot spring over the ground and onto the lake. The flamingos along the shore seem to vanish behind a wall of mist. Occasionally the steam clouds clear and we glimpse ghostly forms paddling in the shallows (77 overleaf).

In the late morning we pack away our cameras and leave the reserve through the Loboi Gate.

MASAI MARA Ⅲ

After leaving Lake Bogoria at the end of May, we drove to Lake Baringo for a few days and then went even farther west to the Uganda border where we

spent two weeks at Mount Elgon National Park. Then it was time to return to Nairobi to replenish our supplies, have the van serviced, and rest for a few days before setting out for our third and final visit to the Masai Mara.

THURSDAY **8** JULY

This morning we leave Nairobi for Masai Mara, but we decide not to go directly to Governor's Camp but instead to make an excursion to Mara Buffalo Camp which is located a few miles outside the reserve on the Mara River. We want to see the largest concentration of hippos in the whole area, estimated at over 200 animals.

5.20pm Just as we turn right off the main track and head towards the camp we see some giraffe heads above a flattish hill. Driving closer we meet the largest herd of giraffes we have ever seen in Kenya (78). We count them three times, and there are twenty-two animals striding across the plain. Unfortunately, they are rather spread out — and Günter cannot get more than ten into one photograph.

We reach the public camp-site at the river just before sunset. Throughout the night we can hear the snorting of hippos from the next river bend upstream.

125

FRIDAY **9** JULY

We drive to the hippo pool before sunrise. The river is very broad and deep where it makes a sharp bend, and opposite us there is a large sandbank — an ideal spot for the hippos. Only a few are on the sand, lying like huge hulks of meat, lazy and indolent. Despite their appearance, hippos can be very fast when they want to be: moreover, they can also be aggressive and unpredictable. Some are covered with

79

scars and scratches. A cow and her fairly large calf look the worst, with several fresh wounds all over the body, a few of which are still bleeding. Yellow-billed oxpeckers and an African pied wagtail clamber over them (79), examining the wounds, which are not caused by fighting, but from acacia thorns while the hippos were feeding during the night.

9.15am All the hippos have now entered the water. In most cases only ears and nostrils are visible. Suddenly two bulls, probably young ones, begin to fight. Heaving their heads and shoulders out of the water, they face each other with mouths wide open to show their tusks. Determined to impress, they dive back into the water and come up once more with open mouths (80). But it is only a minor skirmish, and soon ends. In a serious fight one of the adversaries may be so seriously wounded that it dies of its injuries.

This afternoon we continue driving and enter the Masai Mara through the Musiara Gate, and spend the night at the Crocodile camp-site.

SUNDAY 11 JULY

This morning we visit the marsh. The grass is not as high as it was at this time last year as the 'long rains' in March and April had not been very heavy. A group of zebras waits on top of the hill. Some topis move down to the spring at 7.45am and the zebras follow them.

An hour later a large herd of wildebeest gallops down the slope to drink at the pools by the spring. Some yellow-billed storks are feeding there, constantly moving from one pool to another. Sometimes they just sweep their open bills through the water, or they may hold their open bill in the water while 'stirring' with one foot. They prefer the latter strategy at the water's edge. Some of the storks manage to catch quite large catfish; the rest have to be content with frogs.

9.20am The storks fly away as more and more zebras and wildebeest move down to the spring and spread out across the marsh.

In the afternoon we cross the marsh near Leopard Lugga, where we find the new den of our hyenas — not far from where the old den had been in January. Five females and eight cubs are lying in the sun. One female suckles a single cub, while another feeds two.

5.00pm Two almost completely black cubs emerge from the den and are suckled by a female. Soon afterwards we drive back to the Crocodile camp-site.

MONDAY 12 JULY

Today we meet another group of lions from the Masai pride, by the bend in the river near our camp-site. There are two young males, two young females, and an adult female.

A party of elephants hurries across the plain towards the forest where they will spend the day before coming out again in the evening to feed. In the middle of the elephants we can just see a tiny calf, struggling to keep up. They walk directly towards the lions without seeing them — but the lions move away, running across the camp-site and out of the forest, finally lying down in the tall grass.

Baboons are feeding on the ground at the edge of the forest. One of the young lionesses stalks them, and seconds later the male baboons' warning calls drive the group up into the trees. One male, however, stays on the ground sitting on a termite mound surrounded by banded mongooses. Together they watch the lioness, which gives up after a few minutes and rejoins the others.

Some time later we watch a young female digging out a slender mongoose from its hole. She bites its spine and carries it around. Then she drops it and rejoins the other lions that are resting beneath a tree. Mongoose flesh tastes very strong and although young lions will practise hunting and kill a mongoose, they will not eat it.

Two hyenas come past the mongoose. They sniff at it, and one of them rolls her head and neck on the corpse. They then also move on, leaving it on the ground.

TUESDAY 13 JULY

We drive to the spring to watch the zebras and wildebeest come to drink.

8.30am The wildebeest bulls establish temporary territories in the marsh and try to gather the cows and calves around them. The mating season is over, however, and this activity is much less marked than when the females are in season. The bulls, which are constantly on the move, gallop in circles around their small harems. If two rivals should meet, the result is either a chase or a skirmish, depending on whether one is seeing off an intruder, or whether they happen to meet where their territories meet. Even the zebras keep out of the way of the wildebeest.

WEDNESDAY 14 JULY

8.30am We go to the spring where we find a lioness of the Masai pride hiding in the edge of the high grass. The normal territory of this pride is on the other side of the river. All the animals coming from the northern plains and crossing the stream bed have to pass her. Two juvenile male lions are walking about in the marsh.

9.05am Zebras trek down to the spring from the northern plains. Though they pass some distance away from the lioness, she nevertheless crouches down, seeming to melt into the grass.

After drinking their fill the zebras return the way they have come. A large yearling straggles behind the main herd, passing quite near the lioness. She rises and leaps forward, but gives chase for only a few yards before thinking better of it (81). Shortly afterwards she returns to her hiding place in the grass.

Another group of zebras approaches, but they scent the lioness and take to their heels.

At about midday the lioness decides to move to the edge of the forest. Some zebras and a herd of impalas are also in the forest, but before the lioness can even think of hunting, the impalas sound the alarm. It turns out that eight juvenile lions are the cause: they are lying beneath the trees nearby and have been detected.

The lioness changes her position again, moving to some tall grass between two termite mounds on the other side of the track which the zebras use on their way from the forest to the spring.

3.10pm A group of zebras, which have already passed the lioness unmolested on their way to drink, are making their way back. One of the females has two large open wounds on her hind-quarters. The zebras come quite close to the waiting lioness, and the whole group, including the injured mare, have already passed her when she suddenly jumps up and sprints after them (82 overleaf). It is a long chase, about 200 yards into the forest, but finally the lioness leaps on to the back of the injured mare and brings her to the ground.

The juvenile lions arrive almost immediately and gather round the zebra. The lioness herself leaves the scene and joins the two young males in the marsh. Then all three move to the shade of a tree near the Crocodile camp-site. It is not until 6.00pm when they join the others at the zebra carcass.

MONDAY 19 JULY

6.30am We leave the camp-site to look for some cheetahs that we met yesterday afternoon above Musiara Gate.

'Cheetah' and her two cubs are near Leopard Lugga, resting on a termite mound beside the track. A single Grant's gazelle is grazing in the tall grass by the lugga. Cheetah decides to stalk it. As soon as she gets up her cubs follow, though they are unaware of their mother's intentions and continue playing. But then a hyena approaches the gazelle, which becomes frightened and starts 'strutting'. Cheetah abandons the hunt and returns to the termite mound, where she dozes in the sun with her cubs. At 10.00am the cubs get restless and begin chasing one another. They both try to climb a small acacia, then scuffle on the ground.

2.30pm A herd of impalas, some Tommies, and a bachelor group of Grant's gazelles are grazing on a slope on the opposite side of the lugga.

The four Grant's gazelles move down across the lugga and rest in the grass. After a while they get up and move back. Now Cheetah starts walking towards them, and crouches down behind a tree trunk on the ground.

3.15pm Without any cover she starts to chase the gazelles, which are more than 200 yards away. They spot the danger and flee. At the lugga Cheetah stops and lies down. The cubs join her.

6.00pm The cubs play once more, stalking each other or even their mother. These games teach them different hunting strategies.

WEDNESDAY 21 JULY

6.40am We leave the camp-site and drive to the airstrip, where the two male lions of the airstrip pride are resting in the sun. A lioness and her two cubs are on the other side of the lugga. She frequently lifts her head and stares over the waving grass. Then she gets up and runs towards the lugga, turns back again, and walks out along the track on to the plain. She persuades her cubs to come with her, though they seem unwilling, and mew (83).

We follow as well, and she leads us to the rest of the pride (two sub-adult males, a younger male, and five lionesses), who are gathered round a wildebeest carcass and eating. The newly arrived lioness joins in and her two cubs walk about among their uncles and aunts (84), nibbling here and there at a piece of meat or bone.

FRIDAY 23 JULY

9.30am As soon as we arrive at the spring a herd of zebras races away up the slope. A lioness walks along the marsh towards the spring, and eight other lions of the Masai pride peer curiously out of the grass, awaiting her arrival. They greet each other enthusiastically, then the newcomer lies down with three juveniles on a termite mound. The others stay in the grass.

1.00pm All the lions are now in the tall grass, and some zebras and wildebeest come down the slope. A wildebeest bull comes over to graze at the edge of the grassy area, getting farther away from the herd. Now the lioness spots him and runs parallel with him along the track. Then she breaks into a sprint and cuts off his retreat. After chasing him for about fifty yards she pulls him to the ground with a leap on to his hind quarters.

When we arrive she is about to suffocate the wildebeest. Only his legs are quivering, and then the light dies in his eyes and it is all over. None of the other lions (who are all juveniles) has realized that a hunt has taken place. They were all staring in the other direction at a Masai tribesman approaching with cattle.

After about fifteen minutes a juvenile lioness picks up the scent of the adult and comes to look for her. But, although the adult is sitting up beside her prey, which she has dragged into the tall grass, and staring towards the youngsters, the one who is tracking doesn't see her. With her muzzle close to the ground, she passes about fifteen yards away. Finally she turns round and spies the adult. Then she comes over and both open up the wildebeest's belly and start to eat.

2.30pm The lioness runs over to the juveniles who are still waiting for her. They romp around her, licking her bloody muzzle. Then all of them come to the carcass and eagerly start to eat.

SUNDAY 25 JULY

This morning when we awake there are five well-fed lions lying beside our van. We get up at sunrise, but the lions are still there. Günter carefully opens the sliding door on the other side and steps out. The lions see his feet underneath the van, and rush off into the forest.

After breakfast we leave for the hyena den. It is now at the eastern end of the marsh, not far from Leopard Lugga. It is a large, flattened termite mound with lots of entrance holes.

8.30am Emma is there when we arrive, as well as Ruth, who is suckling her cubs. A young animal about six months old rests at the edge of the den.

Soon a young female arrives from the neighbouring den, about 100 yards away. She heads straight for the resting cub, who immediately lifts its head and shows its teeth. The visiting female bares her teeth too, but backs away. However, for some reason she does not go very far. She waits until the youngster is lying on its side again, then comes forward and grabs the cub by the head, before backing off once more.

The female keeps approaching the cub, but the approaches always end with the showing of teeth on each side, growling, and backing away by the female.

135

During these approaches, the female repeatedly lifts one of her forelegs, which might be a sign of insecurity (85). After several fruitless approaches she manages to grab the cub by the head a second time, but now the youngster gets angry, half rises, and bites back. The female hyena now moves away, her tail down between her legs. She crawls towards Ruth, and when she is close enough suddenly bites her on the backside. Ruth gets up and chases after her.

It is hard to interpret this curious behaviour. All we know is that the female is very young, and has a very low ranking — even lower than most of the juveniles. (This is possible because the social ranking of hyenas follows that of their mothers.) We don't see her very often, and never in any friendly relationship, such as greeting, with other hyenas.

None of the others seems to like or accept her. So maybe she is just trying to find some member, any member, of the clan that is inferior to her — even if it is a young cub.

TUESDAY 27 JULY

During the morning long rows of zebras and wildebeest converge on the marsh. By the early afternoon thousands of wildebeest cover the marsh and the adjacent plains, but compared with those we have observed on previous days the number of zebras is still comparatively small.

We drive to the hyena den at about 4.00pm. Two females and five cubs are lying in front. Through binoculars we can see the lioness Diana at the edge of Fig Tree Forest. She is the individual with the tip of her tail missing, whom we associate with the two sisters; we first met her near Governor's Camp on 13 September last year.

5.00pm Diana gets up, stretches, and walks in the direction of the hyena den. Now and again she stops, looks around, and moves her tail up and down, with the end twitching from side to side. We can tell she is in the mood for hunting.

Wildebeest are leaving the marsh and passing above the hyena den towards Musiara

85

Gate. They have to cross a track, and the cows and calves gallop between two bulls, which have stopped on the track. It is not very hard for Diana to approach through the long grass. Even we can only guess where she is.

Suddenly Diana breaks into the line of wildebeest and kills a calf. The wildebeest swiftly close the gap, as if nothing has happened, and gallop on about thirty yards away from the lioness. She sits up and stares at the wildebeest, then leaves the dead calf on the ground and stalks once more. When she is very close she selects another calf, slightly bigger than the first one.

Diana seizes the calf by the throat. It stands, for about a minute, then she throws it down. For a moment she loosens her grip and stares at the moving column. When the calf begins to struggle she tightens her grasp and kills it. Then she returns to the first animal she has killed, inspects it, and goes back to the second calf where she starts to eat.

6.00pm Another small group of wildebeest passes Diana at a distance of about fifty yards. She looks at them, then leaves her prey and starts to stalk yet again. But this time there is no calf among the wildebeest and they all pass by without her attacking.

7.45am The first wildebeest arrive at the marsh. Soon there are large numbers throughout the area.

In the afternoon it becomes cloudy. Some zebras are grazing along the riverine forest. Then some stallions start to fight. Two of them chase each other from group to group. Often they lose sight of each other, but only for a moment, and then the fighting recommences. They rear up with whirling hooves, trying to grab each other by the neck (86). Elephants are in the marsh feeding, but when it starts to drizzle at about 5.00pm they return to the forest. The zebras fight until sunset.

We go back to the camp-site and make a big fire. On the opposite bank of the river some lions are lying in the open, looking curiously in our direction. When it is dark they start to roar, and receive an answer from a lion on our side of the river. It sounds quite close, but we feel safe in the light of the fire and with the van behind us.

86

The lions roared several times during the night, but by morning they are gone.

We drive to the airstrip and meet Diana coming towards us on the murram road. She lies down behind a termite mound near the culvert. We wait until 9.00am for some prey animal to come close, but then she rolls on her side and dozes in the sun. We leave her, and when we pass by again at 10.00am she has retreated into one of the culverts under the road.

It is about 1.00pm before we look for Diana again. She is now resting on top of the road. A small mixed herd of zebras and wildebeest grazes near the road. They want to come to the pool, but they hesitate. Diana vanishes below the bridge into the reed grass.

3.25pm Finally the animals come towards the water, the zebras in the lead and the wildebeest following behind. But the zebras stop at the edge, allowing the wildebeest to enter the water ahead of them. Now Diana sneaks through the reed grass and veers towards the drinking animals. Some thirty yards away she starts to run, then jumps through the grass into the water, where she surprises a wildebeest calf. Both lioness and calf are standing with only their heads above the water, but Diana is slowly suffocating the calf. Ten minutes later she drags it ashore and starts to feed.

6.30am Cheetah and her two cubs are resting on a termite mound just outside our camp-site. As the sun rises at 6.45am they get to their feet, cross the forest, and walk to the spring where they stop for a drink. They walk on a little farther then settle down in the shade of a bush.

11.00am A number of Masai approach with their cattle, heading towards the river. We watch three other cheetahs that run off at the approach of the Masai. Trying to keep up with them is not easy as they seem to blend in almost completely with the acacia scrub. Finally the three animals — all of them young males — settle down beneath some trees. They are very nervous, and every time a tourist vehicle comes too close they run off. But eventually the other vans drive away, and peace reigns.

In this area, which is outside the reserve, there are many acacia trees, but some bare rocky places, too. By chance we discover an ostrich egg lying forlornly among the rocks. Since it is obviously not in a nest, but an egg that has simply been dropped by a hen, we take it and break it open. The egg is still fresh and makes a wonderful lunch. We even have enough left for our evening meal.

4.30pm For some time nothing has moved except the tips of the cheetahs' tails. But now the cheetahs wake up as clouds cover the sun and it gets cooler. They get up, stretch, and walk to the nearest termite mound to have a look around.

One of them sees a hare and chases it, and the others join in. The hare jinks from side to side, but this doesn't help it much. After a chase of about 100 yards the cheetah catches it. The other two males don't dare come too close, and lie down in the grass at a discreet distance. They get none of the prey, and in a few minutes the hare has disappeared. The one who has eaten goes to a nearby termite mound and lies down. One of the others joins him and licks his muzzle.

A single impala walks past in the distance and the three cheetahs separate, each one trying to approach it from a different angle. We follow one of them which in due course loses contact with his fellows. He sits down on a termite mound and starts to call for them. It is a high, twittering sound like a bird, which we have never heard before. Soon the others find him and all three walk towards the marsh where they try to hunt wildebeest. The hunting attempts are unsuccessful, however, and they give up.

In the morning we go to where we last saw Cheetah and her cubs yesterday morning. They have not moved far, and we find them above the spring in the murram pit. She is resting while the cubs are playing games.

__7.45__am Cheetah gets up and walks onto the ridge. The cubs do not follow right away, playing one more game of catch-me round a boulder. Then they join her, and soon afterwards Cheetah leaves them at a termite mound and goes off to stalk a group of Tommies.

__8.15__am Cheetah gets to within about 100 yards of the herd when the Tommies start to walk away from her, and she stops the hunt. The cubs join Cheetah, who settles down on a termite mound (87), and then they start to chase each other

87

playfully around the mound (88, 89). The family stays on the mound for the next two hours, with occasional breaks for play.

10.45am The cubs suddenly decide to approach our van and investigate. It turns out to be a rather large but fascinating plaything for them. The rubber flaps behind the rear wheels are especially interesting. Cheetah watches them for a while then walks towards them and tries to lead them away by calling. They pay no attention, however, and Cheetah returns to the mound.

11.15am Cheetah moves away, whereupon the cubs stop playing under our van and follow her. They all lie down and doze in the shade of a tree.

1.30pm Cheetah and her cubs get up and walk to the spring, and then on to the plain and towards the gate. They lie down on another termite mound and stare at a Masai approaching with his cattle.

3.00pm Cheetah starts to stalk a group of grazing Tommies. She manages to get relatively close, then crouches

down in the grass and waits for her chance. But suddenly she seems alarmed, turns round and runs back to her cubs. We are puzzled by this abrupt change of heart and so we follow her. We approach and when we arrive Cheetah and her cubs are lying on the ground close together, crying loudly and excitedly, while the three young male cheetahs that we saw yesterday are circling round them, growling (90). Crouched on the bent elbows of their front legs, the males sniff the ground and try to approach Cheetah, who turns her head towards them, growling and crying alternately. The males edge towards her.

One male sniffs for a long time at a spot on the ground, and the others join him. All three are crouching on their elbows sniffing the ground. Suddenly, all six cheetahs disperse in different directions.

Cheetah rejoins her cubs and they settle down close together. The males go straight to where she was lying and sniff the ground. Then they try to approach her again, continually sniffing, while growling and crying again fills the air. And once again they take fright and disperse. Now the cubs are a little apart from their mother, who is obviously in oestrus, and the three males form a semicircle around her hind-quarters. Inch by inch they creep towards her. Cheetah cries at them. The males growl back.

3.40pm The males are still in the same position, as Cheetah will not allow them to come any closer. After a while things calm down and all the cheetahs lie on their sides.

5.45pm We leave the group of cheetahs, which are still lying on the ground in the same position as they were two hours before.

MASAI MARA 1982

TUESDAY 3 AUGUST

We spend the morning near the camp-site, together with a group of eleven lions that are sprawled in the tall grass.

After lunch we go to the airstrip, where we notice that topis, zebras, and wildebeest are all staring in one direction. We follow their gaze and see Cheetah, who is running towards them, followed by her cubs. All the prey animals run away, and Cheetah slows down and stops. For a while she crouches on the track and tries a mock attack on her cubs. Wildebeest are grazing all around as Cheetah and her cubs lie down and rest.

91

2.40pm Cheetah tries to hunt the wildebeest on the left-hand side of the track, but they see her in time and all run away together, so she has no chance. Instead, she runs with her cubs towards the wildebeest on the other side of the track. They panic and the herd splits into two parts, one of which runs up Rhino Ridge. Cheetah chases them for about 100 yards. She stops and she and her cubs settle on a termite mound.

3.25pm Cheetah sits up and looks around. An impala and her young are standing on a termite mound about 200 yards away. The mother is alert and watchful, while the youngster can hardly be seen.

3.40pm Cheetah starts to stalk the impala. The tall grass provides perfect cover, At about 100 yards range, Cheetah stops and stares for some minutes at the impala, which has her back turned to Cheetah and is looking in the other direction.

3.55pm Cheetah stalks forward again. The impala sees her at the last minute and races away with her youngster. The rest of the impala herd, who are not far away at the edge of a small patch of forest, make their getaway as well, jumping between and over bushes with graceful leaps and bounds. But the young impala proves an easy target, and Cheetah catches it after about 150 yards. The mother stops and runs back, but Cheetah is already carrying the dead animal to her cubs, who are coming to meet her.

The cubs crouch down, then sneak around their mother trying to grab the impala (91). Cheetah carries it for another 100 yards, then drops it and the cubs take it over. First they drag it in a circle around their mother, then they start to eat. Cheetah joins them after about ten minutes, first pulling the carcass onto a nearby termite mound.

After a while Cheetah stops eating and lies down to rest. Two legs are all that remains of the young impala, and the cheetah cubs play tug of war with them.

4.30pm We return to the marsh, and find that the lions are still where we left them this morning — eleven lions distributed among three termite mounds. The juveniles start to play in the late afternoon, when it becomes cooler. They lie in wait for each other, sometimes jumping into the air to counter an attack, sometimes fighting on the ground. It is all good practice for the day when they will have to hunt for themselves.

WEDNESDAY 4 AUGUST

The eleven lions of the Masai pride are still outside our camp-site. A lioness sets off in pursuit of a buffalo, then pauses to wait for her companions to join in. As none of them show any interest she abandons the idea.

7.00am A solitary wildebeest bull is crossing the marsh. The lions soon spot him, and all eleven set off in line abreast through the long grass. One lioness crouches flat on the track and seems to melt into the ground. The bull walks towards her. But when he is only yards away a juvenile starts to chase him, coming sideways at him through the grass. The wildebeest turns away and escapes.

Now all the lions trot to the edge of the marsh, and the younger ones start to play in the pools. Before long some other vehicles arrive on the scene and we return to the camp-site.

2.30pm When we return in the afternoon the lions are sprawled out on a large termite mound. We leave them for a time, coming back at 4.00pm. By now they have moved to the fig trees near Fig Tree Forest. One lioness is on a termite mound, the rest are in the grass. Buffalos are grazing only 200 yards away but the lions don't bother about them. Clouds are gathering in the east and build up into a thunderstorm. Now the lions have all woken up, and one after another join the lioness on the mound. The sky is almost completely black, and only a few rays of sun break through.

5.30pm Some marabous drop from the sky and land at the edge of Fig Tree Forest pool. The lions can see that more and more marabous are arriving, but they cannot see what is going on because of the long grass. So they get up and run towards the birds in a long line. One can almost read the expectation in their faces. But any thoughts of an easy meal are replaced by evident frustration when they arrive at the pool and realize that the marabous are not gathering round a carcass but simply fishing. There are about thirty birds, and the lions sit watching them with puzzled looks.

It starts to drizzle and we drive back to the camp-site.

THURSDAY 5 AUGUST

7.20am A male and a female ground hornbill perch on a dead tree at the edge of the marsh, calling to each other in turn. Their repetitive but melodious calls somewhat resemble those of a hoopoe. We name the pair Caesar and Cleopatra. In fact, Cleopatra is a very privileged bird, for she lives with two males.

The second male, whom we call Cicero, is with Cleopatra's offspring Benjamin at the moment. Benjamin is about to examine a hole in the tree trunk. Then Cicero spots some elephant dung nearby and flies down to it, followed by Benjamin. Together the two hornbills stir up the dung in their search for beetles and other choice items. Caesar and Cleopatra break off their duet and join them.

7.35am When the family have thoroughly searched the dung, they walk on along the edge of the marsh. The rather clumsy, turkey-sized birds stride leisurely through the tall grass and reeds, apparently on the lookout for frogs. Their big dark eyes, which are protected by very long lashes, miss nothing. Now there is a frog struggling in Caesar's beak. He gives it a quick, elegant swing, and opens his beak wide, and the frog flies through the air and vanishes down Caesar's throat (92).

7.50am A little while later the family meets a pair of Egyptian geese grazing at the edge of the marsh. Young Benjamin apparently wants to play with them and runs forward with wings spread wide. The geese, who are barely half as big as the ground hornbills, retreat onto the water. But Benjamin doesn't give up. Again and again he flies low over their heads, chasing the cackling geese here and there until they finally take off and fly away (93).

FRIDAY 6 AUGUST

This morning we leave camp well before dawn, with only a hunter's moon to show us the way. As the first morning light touches the long grass it turns to gold. Wildebeest move down on to Paradise Plain and become black dots in a golden sea. We take the track to Kiboko Crossing, and where the grass is shorter we come across Cheetah and her two cubs. We follow them all morning.

12.00am Cheetah trots towards four Thomson's gazelles grazing in the tall grass. At 100 yards Cheetah starts to stalk and the cubs which have been following stay behind. At fifty yards, Cheetah crouches behind a clump of grass.

The Tommies move directly towards her. The closer they get, the lower Cheetah crouches. Finally, when the leading gazelle is only about ten yards away, Cheetah leaps from her cover. The Tommy jumps straight up in the air, turns a somersault, and starts running as soon as he is on his feet. With Cheetah at his heels he runs from side to side, then makes a turn and doubles back.

All three cheetahs finally catch the gazelle. Cheetah seizes him by the throat, while the cubs jump up at their mother. Cheetah drags the body for a few yards, then leaves it to her cubs. One grabs its throat while the other tries to open its hind-quarters. The Tommy is still alive and starts to move, whereupon the cub holding its throat releases it and the Tommy lifts its head. But the young cheetah seizes hold again.

The mother does not interfere, though the cubs look at her as if they don't know quite what to do next. Finally they despatch the gazelle, and after dragging it round in a circle they settle down to eat.

1.50pm Cheetah and one cub have apparently finished their meal, and come out. We drive away carefully and return to the camp-site.

8.05am A family of wart hogs — two adults and two juveniles — are walking about near the spring by the marsh. The young ones wallow in a muddy hole while the adults drink from a ditch. In a few minutes the adult wart hogs simply jump over the ditch and move on up the slope. The young ones immediately follow, leaving the mud-bath and leaping the ditch in turn (94).

8.20am We drive about 100 yards along the marsh to a stretch of open water where six yellow-billed storks are fishing (95). The birds walk slowly forwards, at the same time scything their half-open beaks from side to side through the water in front of their legs. As soon as they touch something that feels like a fish they close their beaks immediately. They don't catch many fish, but when they do it is worth it. None of the fish seem to be smaller than nine inches long. They are all catfish, as no other species can live in the marsh which dries out for some months each year.

When one of the storks catches a fish it leaves the water to get away from its companions. It prefers to consume the fish undisturbed, as this can take a long time.

9.15am The storks feed for at least an hour, then leave the water to preen, standing close together on the shore. We leave them and drive on along the marsh, then cross over towards Fig Tree Forest where there is another marsh. Here, too, there are

They eat only for a short time, however, for it is very hot, and one after the other come across to our van and lie down underneath it. Now Cheetah starts to eat. But before long she joins her cubs under the van.

1.10pm One of the youngsters goes over to the prey and proceeds to drag it to the van. Cheetah and the other cub join in, but soon Cheetah takes it away from the cubs and pulls it under the van on her own. All three cheetahs are now under the van, eating contentedly — while we remain hungry, and baking in the sun.

95

some open stretches of water where yellow-billed storks and great white egrets are fishing. A large saddle-billed stork strides through the reeds in search of frogs.

In one of the larger pools a party of zebras is standing in the knee-deep water. They are drinking, but they are very nervous, for the water hinders them if they need to escape — and all around them lions could be lurking. From time to time they dash through the water for no obvious reason (96). But they soon calm down again and resume drinking.

After a while they have quenched their thirst and move on to the land, leaving a pathway of churned-up, muddy water behind them.

MONDAY 9 AUGUST

Kiboko Crossing is an open stretch of the Mara River with a few palm trees, but no forest, along the banks. First Crossing lies below the Two Hills, where the river is still meandering through riverine forest. It is a long narrow cut without vegetation, where the ground is covered with stones and boulders. It leads into the forest and thence to the river. We guess that these two crossings will soon become very busy and filled with wildebeest.

Sometimes the wildebeest arrive overnight in thousands and spread out on Paradise Plain. Today is such a day. The wildebeest are everywhere. All Paradise is full of them. From Rhino Ridge to Paradise Hill more and more pour down onto the plain. And all have but one aim, to head for one of the crossing points on the Mara River, in order to trek back to the Serengeti plains on their annual migration in search of fresh food and water.

We drive to the forest near First Crossing and stop the van. A line of bushes stands between us and the wildebeest, but we can hear them and a few minutes later they start to cross.

150

7.45am Soon we can see them on the other side. Now we move forward through the bushes until we reach the crossing point. Here access to the water is easy, but the bank opposite is steep, and most of the animals gather there, trying to climb or jump up. In fact, the only way up is not here but farther downstream. The animals discover this by following others as they swim down following the bank.

The crossing is halted for a couple of hours when some vehicles appear on the other bank, and the wildebeest in the river turn back and stampede onto the plain.

10.30am A herd of wildebeest appears on top of the bank on the other side. Seeing them, the wildebeest on our side enter the river again. Presently the whole herd is pushing forward. The animals are entering the water some yards away, but soon we are surrounded by them.

We stay watching them crossing the river,

and the various problems they encounter, and then return to the camp at 11.30 am.

4.00pm In the afternoon we drive out to Paradise Plain for a while, but we want to get back to the camp-site early as we plan to roast a leg of lamb. We sit down to eat in the van, leaving the rest of the meat on the fire. When we go over to fetch a second helping the lamb has disappeared. It was probably stolen by a hyena.

TUESDAY 10 AUGUST

3.45pm This afternoon we go to Paradise Plain again. Down in the depression where there are a number of solitary acacias, a large buffalo herd is grazing. The animals are spread over a large area. A forbidding-looking wall of thunder clouds is approaching from the east. It is a wonderful sight, with the bulky black bodies of the buffalo standing in the golden grass with a heavy, dark sky as a background (97). But we cannot stay very long for we are some miles from our camp-site, and if we are caught by the rain it is possible that we may be unable to drive back.

4.20pm The first rain drops fall shortly before we reach Governor's Camp, but the sun is still shining. A group of female waterbuck, led by a big male, is standing at the edge of the forest (98 overleaf). Rain or no rain, we drive over to take some photographs of them as they stand there, indifferent to the downpour, the sun making the droplets glitter and shine. Then we hurry to the camp. Fortunately, although the ground is wet, it is not yet very slippery.

SATURDAY **14** AUGUST

*3.15pm We go to Para-
dise Plain, but the wildebeest have left and the
plains are empty. There is nothing but golden
grass as far as the eye can see.*

*On our way back via Rhino Ridge we meet
Cheetah and her two cubs lying in the shade*
*of an acacia. Cheetah is staring straight
ahead, a sure sign that she is ready to hunt.
Soon she sets out with the cubs following
behind. But numerous mini-buses arrive and
drive in front of Cheetah so that their passengers can get close enough to take photographs of her. This disturbs her hunting and
she gives up and lies on a termite mound. She
is still there when we leave at 5.30pm.*

99

7.45am We find Cheetah and her cubs on the other side of Rhino Ridge. The cubs are playing, and this brings them towards the van. As they chase each other, one of the cubs jumps up, leans inside, and plays with the camera on the tripod which is fixed to the door. More vehicles arrive and

after a while Cheetah becomes nervous and leads the cubs away.

3.30pm Quite suddenly all three cheetahs chase a banded mongoose which escapes up into a small acacia tree. It clings to a branch while the cubs try to climb the tree. But Cheetah just looks up, then wanders away. The cubs join her after a while, having failed to reach the mongoose. But although the cheetahs go, the mongoose stays up in the tree.

5.30pm Near to Kiboko Crossing Cheetah tries to stalk a group of Tommies and topis, but gives up when some cars and mini-buses approach. The cubs decide to explore the encircling vehicles. One jumps on to a bonnet, from where it is not far to the roof. Minutes later the two cubs are gnawing at the canvas top. Cheetah gets agitated and calls to the cubs. The driver also tries to get rid of them by starting his engine. They take no notice of all this, and even stay in place when the car begins to move. But now they feel uncomfortable and jump off.

SATURDAY **21** AUGUST

5.30am We leave our camp-site in the dark so that we can be ready in position at the jackal den up on Topi Plain by the time the sun rises.

We cross the airstrip lugga and drive up the slope, when we meet the lions of the airstrip pride. They are lying sleepily around a termite mound, apparently waiting for the sun. A blood-red sky in the east announces that the sunrise is on its way.

Günter opens the door of the van and lies down on the ground with his camera, as he wants to photograph the lions' heads silhouetted against the morning sky (99). But this seems to arouse the lions' curiosity, and they get up one after another and start to walk in our direction. Günter quickly gets back in and we drive on to the jackal den. It is a big earthy termite mound, and when we get there the sun is just rising above the horizon.

6.45am One adult black-backed jackal and five cubs are lying in front of the den. The cubs are about six weeks old and a bit shy. They vanish inside when we arrive, while the adult walks a few yards and lies down again. We drive a short distance farther away before settling down to watch.

*6.50*am *Within minutes a tiny head appears at the entrance hole (100). Cautiously the young jackal looks around, then retreats back into the safety of the den. Several times we see a tiny head peering out of the entrance hole before the cubs apparently decide that we pose no danger to them. Then they come out one after another and start to play (101).*

*7.30*am *Another adult arrives at the den. The cubs run over to greet him, and push again and again at his muzzle to stimulate him to regurgitate food. After he has done this, the male lies down near the den. The cubs start to play again. At times two pairs might be scuffling, while the fifth cub disappears into the den. Then an alarm call sounds and the playing ends abruptly. All of the cubs vanish inside and don't reappear.*

MONDAY 23 AUGUST

7.30am Wildebeest cover the plains and the slopes of Rhino Ridge. We drive to Paradise Plain, and then follow the track to the crossing. A male and female lion are lying just before the cut through the forest. (They belong to the Paradise pride, whose two males are the most handsome lions we have met in the Mara: the one we see now is the one with the lighter mane.)

The pair is resting, with the female lying on her side next to the male (102). After a few minutes she gets up and walks a short distance. The male gets up immediately and follows her.

When the female crouches slightly the male mounts (103).

When the copulation is nearly ended the lioness turns her head towards her mate and growls, baring her teeth (104). The male leaves her quickly, but she does not bite him. She then rolls on to her back, stretching all four legs in the air. After this both lions rest, and all is quiet.

8.40am We drive on to Kiboko Crossing, where a herd of wildebeest, led by some topis, are running towards the river. They stop when they reach the bank, but the pressure of new animals arriving behind them is building up all the time. The wildebeest at the front are nervous, but suddenly a calf jumps into the water, which triggers the others to take the plunge too. The crossing has begun (105).

We watch for a while, and then drive back along Rhino Ridge, where we come across a newly dead wildebeest. We are the first to discover the carcass, so we wait until the inevitable scavengers arrive. It is fantastic to watch the first vultures dropping from the sky. With wings outstretched, they strut screaming towards the carcass and try to tear it open. Some even land directly on the wildebeest. First they attack the anus, as the skin elsewhere is too tough for their beaks.

More and more vultures arrive, and each newcomer fights to get a place, perhaps by pecking vigorously at the back of an earlier

arrival. Sometimes one seizes another by the neck or shoulder, and throws it on its back. The one on its back is now in a submissive position, so the victor immediately leaves him and turns to the melee round the carcass.

2.30pm Most of the vultures take to the air on the afternoon breeze. We leave too, and spend the rest of the afternoon with the ground hornbills.

163

2.40pm The lugga near the First Crossing has nearly dried up, but there are still some muddy pools, and in one of them we see three old buffalo bulls. They are almost completely covered in a thick layer of mud, which no doubt gives some protection against ticks and flies (106). We come close, and one gets up and shakes his head, causing great lumps of mud to fly off.

Elsewhere some marabous are fishing. This seems to be a good spot, as others fly in from all directions (107). But in a few days time this pool will have dried up too.

A monitor lizard swims between the legs of the marabous. One of the birds pecks at the lizard's tail, and the lizard retaliates by turning round and grabbing the beak of the startled bird. But the lizard seems to consider discretion the better part of valour, and climbs on to a small island where it hides in the grass.

107

THURSDAY 26 AUGUST

8.00am *Driving along the road to Little Governor's Camp we come upon two lionesses and three six-month-old cubs, probably part of the Masai pride. As we approach they get up and walk to the road, then trot along ahead of us for a while. But then one of the lionesses leaves the road and starts stalking a group of wart hogs, using a large termite mound for concealment. The wart hogs (one female and her young ones) are grazing about thirty yards away where the grass is short.*

The lioness hides behind the termite mound and waits. Sometimes we catch a glimpse of her peering round the side (108). Meanwhile the other lioness has walked farther along the road with the cubs.

The wart hogs move slowly towards the road, the youngster in front and the female following. They pass the termite mound and are nearly at the road. The lioness now comes into the open and follows them. The young wart hogs see her and start running, but their mother only trots. Still the following lioness does not accelerate, for by not scaring the wart hogs she is driving them straight to the second lioness, who is hiding in the long grass on the other side of the road.

Suddenly the second lioness leaps out and grabs the female wart hog by the neck. The wart hog defends herself vigorously, but the lioness's grip is firm and she drags the kicking animal into the grass. Now the first lioness arrives and seizes the wart hog's hind-quarters, while the other one still holds on to the throat and starts to suffocate it (109).

The struggling wart hog manages to kick the first lioness on the snout (110). She is startled and grimaces. The cubs approach, but one of the females growls and swipes at them with a paw, and they back away.

The lioness at the front momentarily loosens her grip and the wart hog tries to escape. But she is quickly caught. After ten minutes the lionesses change places, and the one who is now at the hind-quarters starts to eat. Once more the cubs come up but this time they are allowed to stay, and they start to eat as well.

The wart hog is still alive and kicking, and once again the lionesses swap places, with the one who had been eating, taking her turn

108

at suffocating (111). The wart hog finally dies half an hour after the beginning of the hunt.

9.20*am One of the lionesses leaves the prey and lies down on the road. Ten minutes later another lioness arrives and goes to the carcass.*

SATURDAY **28** AUGUST

8.30*am We watch five hyenas hunting wildebeest near Fig Tree Forest. One of them runs towards a grazing herd, to divide it into two as the animals run away. A wildebeest calf stands undecided between the two groups, which gives the hyena her chance. She waits for the others to join her, and they chase the calf for fifty yards. It tries to defend itself with its horns, but one of the hyenas throws it to the ground. It gets up when a passing mini-bus distracts the hyenas. But once more they get it down.*

Other hyenas arrive, until six are at the baby wildebeest, with four more waiting nearby. They are not very hungry, and even though they gnaw at its hind-quarters, the calf gets to its feet yet again. But they catch it and continue gnawing. It is still alive, but finally dies after fifteen minutes.

TUESDAY 31 AUGUST

7.00am Near the culvert under the road we meet one of the two sisters. Concealed in tall grass the lioness is tracking a wart hog in parallel, hoping to cut it off. But when the wart hog starts to trot she gives up.

The lioness walks out onto the plain in a big circle, and eventually lies down in some grass. She is facing into the wind — and also towards a group of seven wart hogs (two adults and five youngsters). The lioness creeps forward and then crouches down when she is about thirty yards away from the wart hogs. One of the adults comes towards her and starts to graze at the very clump of grass that she is hiding behind. But still the lioness waits.

8.50am She leaps forward, aiming at the group and disregarding the wart hog next to her. The wart hogs scatter and she chases one of them, but soon gives up. She rests on a termite mound for a while, then sets out for the riverine forest. We follow.

A herd of wildebeest is galloping towards the river, parallel to the edge of the forest. The leading animals are nervous about something, and change course. Then they stop, and run back, making a wide detour round the area which has aroused their suspicion.

9.40am The lioness is now about 100 yards from the wildebeest and is starting to stalk. The grass is still tall, and we lose sight of her. We drive closer, trusting to luck. As we stop, the lioness jumps up about thirty yards from us and breaks into the line of wildebeest. She clings to the neck of an adult male with her front paws — a deadly embrace (112).

114

The wildebeest turns (113 previous pages) and moves about (114), but after two minutes it is on the ground. Three minutes later it is dead (115). After a brief pause to catch her breath the lioness bites into her prey between its hind-legs. Then she seizes it by the head and drags it towards the forest (116).

10.00am The lioness stops for breath after a few yards, then carries on towards the trees.

10.20am She reaches the forest. We return to our camp-site.

115

FRIDAY 3 SEPTEMBER

We leave the camp-site at Governor's Camp an hour before sunrise, while it is still dark, and head for the hyena den at Musiara Swamp. The eastern sky seems to burn, just for a few seconds, about half an hour before sunrise. Then day begins to dawn while the full moon is still visible over the Siria Escarpment. Some topis are resting in the grass beside the track.

6.15am We have reached the den, but only a few hyenas are present. Emma is lying out in front. A one-year-old approaches the den and greets Emma, who takes no notice. Then the juvenile goes down the entrance hole and emerges with Emma's two five-week-old cubs. The cubs and the juvenile start playing together.

The twins are very inquisitive and move away from the entrance to explore the surroundings. Emma and the juvenile follow them when they have gone about ten feet, as they are still very small and awkward. Reaching the cubs, the two older animals turn them round with their noses and push them back towards the den. Once they are safely back by the den, Emma lies down and the cubs resume playing.

7.00am About one mile away three lionesses are coming down the hill near Musiara Gate. It is Diana and the two sisters. We keep an eye on them, but stay with the hyenas. The lionesses pass about 300 yards from the den, and keep on walking alongside the track. After another quarter of a mile they lie down in the grass.

8.00am The lionesses are moving about in an odd way, but as we cannot see what is going on, even through binoculars, we drive over to have a closer look. The three lionesses are lying around a flattish termite mound and taking turns at digging at a hole. Sometimes they stop and stare intently into the hole. Suddenly one of them starts to dig rapidly followed by the other two. We assume that a wart hog is hiding inside.

8.30am Diana withdraws a few yards and rolls on to her back, with all four legs in the air. But the sisters continue

117

staring into the hole. We move the van to photograph Diana — but have hardly come to a halt when there is a sudden frenzy of activity. Diana jumps through the air, while the other two are whirling round trying to catch a full-grown wart hog. One manages to get hold of it by the neck and another by the throat. The wart hog puts up a furious fight and is making a lot of noise, but the big cats have a firm hold. Two minutes later the wart hog is lying on the ground and two of the lionesses start to bite into its stomach and hind-legs. But it is still alive, so the third lioness grabs it by the throat again to suffocate it.

When the wart hog's stomach is opened up, the third one joins the other two. The lionesses are eating very hastily, stopping only for a quick look around, then back to their meal.

Ten minutes after the kill, the first two hyenas come from the den, followed by several others. They first skirt the lionesses in a big semi-circle, then slowly advance with tails raised in aggression and growling loudly (117). They become increasingly daring as some more hyenas join them.

Now the phalanx of eight hungry hyenas is so close that the animals are almost touching the lionesses' muzzles. Suddenly the lionesses leave the carcass to the hyenas, and move away without offering any resistance. One hyena follows them for a few paces, then turns back to join her fellows. There are now about twenty hyenas present, and within seconds they are tearing the wart hog to pieces (118).

(Later, on returning home, we were looking through the photographs and noticed that one of the hyenas has a pink foetus in its mouth: the wart hog had been pregnant.)

The lionesses are sitting only a few yards away, licking the blood from their paws and paying no attention to the hyenas.

After five minutes one of the hyenas runs off with a wart hog leg.

118

9.00am Now only the head of the wart hog remains. Emma picks it up and carries it back to the den (119). The lionesses seek the shade of a solitary acacia.

Neither hyenas nor lions had had much to eat for the last three days. The plains were empty as many wildebeest had already crossed the river on their way back to the Serengeti. It will take a few more days for the next wave of the migrating animals to arrive.

Masai Mara 1982
MASAI MARA 1982

FRIDAY **10** SEPTEMBER

We visit the jackals' den before sunrise. One adult is lying in front while the cubs are having a wonderful time, chasing around and biting each other's tails.

At about 7.00am two more adults arrive at the den. The cubs run up to the newcomers with tails wagging and push against their muzzles. Then the youngsters lie on their backs and the adults regurgitate food for them. After they have eaten, the cubs disappear inside the den and the adults settle down and doze.

We drive to the river crossings, and spend some hours watching the comings and goings of wildebeest. At 3.30pm we set off again for Rhino Ridge, where we encounter a giraffe with a newly born baby among the rocks (120). The baby was probably born that morning as it is already dry and can walk.

SATURDAY **11** SEPTEMBER

3.30pm We go to see what is happening at the hyena den. There are wildebeest everywhere in the marsh and the adjacent plains, all slowly making their way towards Paradise and the river crossings. The only place they avoid is the immediate vicinity of the hyena den. However, hyenas are already wandering about among the wildebeest.

Four hyenas have killed a wildebeest calf about fifty yards from the den, perhaps five minutes before our arrival. But they don't seem at all hungry and are only picking at the carcass in a desultory way. They did not need to kill the calf, but no doubt the sight of thousands of wildebeest milling about around their den simply aroused their hunting instincts. The calf may have been sick or behaving abnormally, and so attracted their attention.

One of the four hyenas is Emma, who soon leaves the calf and returns to the den. She has noticed her twin cubs straying farther than she would like, so she picks up one and takes it back to the den with the other trotting along beside her (121).

Now some vultures appear, and stand around waiting for the hyenas to move away from the young wildebeest. But some juvenile hyenas have seen them landing and come over to see what is going on. One of them, about four months old, behaves as if he has never seen a vulture before. Half fearful, half curious, he cautiously approaches one of these strange creatures (122). The vulture does not move until the young hyena is almost touching its beak. But then it apparently feels threatened. It spreads its wings and pecks at the youngster, which gets a fright and jumps back.

More hyenas are now arriving from the marsh, where they have been resting in muddy pools. Most have not seen the hunting, but are attracted by the sight of gathering vultures. The last to arrive is Eve with her two cubs, by now nearly one year old. She is a very high-ranking female and takes over the prey at once. She and her cubs drive all the others away, allowing only one juvenile to remain behind.

5.00pm Only the head, fur, and spine of the wildebeest are left. A thunderstorm is approaching from the east, and we drive back to our camp-site.

7.45am On our way to the jackal den we come across a dying wildebeest calf. It is already too weak to get up, and lies on the ground waiting for death. Other wildebeest pass by in the distance and the calf looks wistfully after them, struggling vainly to get to its feet and join them.

An adult jackal arrives and tears at the hind-quarters of the calf, which is unable to defend itself. But the jackal is obviously not hungry and soon lies down nearby. Finally it walks back to the den, marking its way by urinating as it goes.

10.15am We drive to Paradise Plain, where long columns of wildebeest are trekking towards the crossing points. There is a tree just beside the cut leading to the First Crossing, and most of the wildebeest pause here before entering the forest. We are keen to photograph the massed wildebeest from a vantage point, so we experiment with fixing a camera in the tree so that we can operate it from a distance with a radio signal.

It seems to work, so we plan to come back and repeat it when there are more wildebeest. At 2.30pm we return to the camp-site.

WEDNESDAY 15 SEPTEMBER

6.45am The area between Two Hills and the Mara River is black with wildebeest, and more flow down from the slopes — hundreds and thousands merging into a teeming mass. The huge herd moves slowly but surely towards the cut leading through the forest to the river. This is one of their favourite crossing points.

But today there is a problem in the shape of four lions — three males and a female —

which are lying just by the cut and blocking access to the river (123). They are well-fed and lazy, and unconcerned by what is going on around them. They don't even glance at the solid wall of wildebeest, now only 100 yards away.

We drive to the tree, which Günter climbs to fix the camera in position, while I keep an eye on the lions.

The lions get up and move into some bushes at 7.30am, but the wildebeest are still nervous, and hesitate to enter the cut. Finally, at 8.40am, they overcome their fears and start moving forwards (124). Günter triggers the camera by radio several times, and then we hurry to reach the river.

We drive to where we expect the wildebeest will enter the water and we stop between some bushes. The thunder of hooves and continual bellowing sound like waves breaking on a distant shore. This noise gradually gets louder. The wildebeest are coming.

The first animals come into sight and run along the river's edge. In no time the narrow stretch of bare ground between the river and the bank is packed with wildebeest. There must be hundreds of them, but we hear more than we can see because they quickly stir up a thick cloud of dust (125 overleaf). The animals are very excited and nervous, and constantly dash to and fro.

Soon some apparently deserted calves

appear at the top of the steep bank on the other side of the river, attracted by all the noise. They have probably crossed the river earlier, and somehow lost contact with their mothers. Now they are running about, bellowing excitedly and hoping to find their mothers again.

The wildebeest on our side of the river hesitate, unable to decide whether to enter the water. But the calves on the other side cannot wait any longer. One after another they jump from the steep bank, which is ten to fifteen feet high (126), down into the river, and swim across to plunge into the wildebeest massed on the shore.

The first wildebeest eventually enter the water where it is very shallow. Once they have made a move, the ones behind surge forward, blindly putting their trust in those in front. Within seconds a broad line of wildebeest is pouring into the river.

The urge to reach the river is so strong that some animals from the back of the herd swing out sideways and come through the bushes beside our van in order to get there quicker. But the bank here is much steeper, and the only way down is to jump. Some do this, plunging fearlessly into the swirling water below (127).

It is an easy swim across the river, for it is only forty yards wide and the current is not

126

very strong. The problem is on the other side. The banks there, like almost everywhere along this river, are very high and steep. In a stretch of about 300 yards there is only one place where they can conveniently climb out. Even this is not much — just a steep, narrow track where the bank has been trampled by hippos. It is a curious fact that all the traditional crossing places have easy access into the water, but not out of it.

By now hundreds of wildebeest have reached the opposite side. Some swim in a compact mass upstream, looking for a way out, while others try to climb up just where they have arrived. It is a difficult spot. Other wildebeest have tried to get out here on previous days, and some have made it. But today it is hardly passable, due to the thousands of hooves that have already worn away the bank. Nevertheless, the wildebeest are determined to try (128). Most of them fall back into the heaving, shoving throng below.

Meanwhile, more and more wildebeest are entering the river, which is now half-filled with heads and horns. Some weaker ones never make it across. Again and again we see heads vanishing beneath the water without coming up again. Others lose their determination, break away from their fellows, and try to swim back.

But now some animals on the other side have firm ground under their feet and walk along the shore, heading upstream towards the exit (129). This is about fifty yards away, and although it is not steep, it is narrow and strewn with rocks.

The first animals have reached the exit and stagger upwards, exhausted. A queue builds up on the bank, as the wildebeest make for the way out. Soon the narrow path is blocked by the milling horde (130 overleaf). Summoning their last reserves of strength they fight to stay on their feet. One by one they stumble up the bank and gallop away onto the plain. Some, however, are not so lucky, especially the young and the weak. Many lose their footing, fall to the ground, and are instantly trampled to death.

9.30am The crossing is over. Most of the wildebeest — 2,000 or more — have managed to climb the bank, but several hundred are still on our side of the river. A few confused stragglers stand tired and forlorn at the foot of the exit. And everywhere we can see bodies of those who failed. Carcasses litter the opposite bank and lie half-submerged in the river itself. Vultures and marabous have already arrived to take advantage of the feast (131). What is tragedy for some some is a blessing for others.

9.00am The First Crossing is again blocked by lions, but this time the wildebeest turn away and walk up the hill towards Kiboko Crossing.

Behind the hill sprawl the rest of the lion pride — one male and three females. They are not hungry, however, and show no interest in the passing wildebeest. Some time goes by before one of the lionesses notices a sick calf. The youngster stands alone and motionless among some rocks, staring at the herd it can no longer follow because it is too weak to keep pace. Such an easy prey is enough to awaken the hunting instincts of even the most satiated lion.

So she gets up and walks in a straight line towards the rocks, followed soon afterwards by the other two lionesses. The calf is still facing the herd and, although the other wildebeest snort with alarm when they see the lions, the calf does not turn round until the first lioness is almost upon it.

The calf lowers its horns and the lioness shrinks back slightly — but then swipes at the calf with her paw. Meanwhile, the other two lionesses have reached the calf and they too strike it with their paws, almost playfully, as domestic cats do when playing with a mouse. When the calf finally falls to the ground, one of the lionesses grabs it by the throat while the other two continue playing with it, pushing it this way and that with their paws (132). The one holding its throat loosens her grip for a moment and the calf gets to its feet. But seconds later it is brought down again with several powerful slaps.

Now one lioness grabs the calf by the neck and pulls it to its feet. The next moment it is down again, and one of the lionesses grabs its throat and starts to suffocate it. The other two gnaw at its hind-quarters.

9.45am It has taken half an hour, but the lionesses have finally killed the calf. Now the male lion approaches and the lionesses retreat leaving him the carcass.

FRIDAY **17** SEPTEMBER

Today is our last day in the Masai Mara. We drive out to say goodbye to some of our friends. First we visit the jackals. The cubs are growing up, and are already the same colour as the adults, though they are still smaller.

They are now venturing as far as fifty yards from the den.

We move on to Rhino Ridge, where we meet Cheetah and her two cubs. We decide to spend the rest of the day with them. In the late afternoon Cheetah goes hunting, but without success.

Tomorrow we shall leave for Nairobi, and then home.

AUTHOR'S NOTE

Every zoologist and ethologist must dream of travelling to Africa. After I had completed my studies at the University of Munich my own dream came true when Günter offered me the chance to join him on his next trip to Kenya. At last I could put aside my textbooks, exercise my knowledge and make observations for myself while studying animal behaviour at first-hand.

Günter and I share the same interests, but we pursue them in different ways. He uses his camera to record the way animals behave while I observe their activities, trying to understand and interpret what I see in scientific terms. But a great deal of time, patience and perseverance is needed by both of us.

Our trip to Africa provided an opportunity to see wildlife in its natural habitat, and to understand the interdependence of species. Following my first lion making a kill was such a fascinating and exciting experience that I felt no discomfort from the broken tooth that resulted from an unexpected jolt of our van.

My parents, who had noted my concern for wild animals as a child when I regularly cared for sick and injured individuals, found it hard to understand my apparent lack of sympathy for the victims of predators. But in the wilderness life is cheap and death is commonplace, being simply part and parcel of nature's cycle, and more readily acceptable when one is in the wild and can identify with it. And there we were; in a fever of excitement, watching the hunts of hyenas, lions and cheetahs, observing the vultures as they tore carcasses to pieces, hearing the roar of lions at night, from near at hand, and listening to the exquisite bird songs.

The animal that really entranced me, however, was a big, black and ugly bird — the ground hornbill — with its characteristically strange behaviour. Polygyny (when a male has more than one mate at a time) is well known among many species, but polyandry (when a female has more than one mate) is this bird's speciality. Initially I had to encourage Günter's interest in these birds and he is still less fond of them than I am, but his photographer's curiosity was stimulated by their strange behaviour, and we spent many happy hours together watching the ground hornbill. The sound of their voices at dawn and the proud progress of the family across the plains are for me unforgettable memories.

While observing and writing, I often forgot that I had a camera myself. I made entries every day in my diary, and our year in Africa resulted in literally hundreds of observations, noted briefly at the time on paper or by using a tape recorder, later being written up more explicitly. The text of this book is closely associated with the pictures in order to assist appreciation of the circumstances in which each photograph was taken. I hope that the book may also encourage the reader to undertake his own safari and see for himself the wonders of the African wilderness. I would be very happy if our book helped to spread an understanding of the natural world, and concern for its life and landscape, which we have a duty to preserve for our children.

Angelika Hofer Füssen 1984

HOUSE ACKNOWLEDGMENTS

Editorial Director   Ian Jackson
Art Editor   Nigel Partridge
Cartographic Editor   Caroline Simpson
Map Artist   Andrew Farmer
Proof Reader   Jocelyn Selson

Eddison/Sadd Editions acknowledge with
grateful thanks the assistance received from
Bruce Coleman throughout the production of
this book. Günter Ziesler's photographs
appear here by arrangement with
Bruce Coleman Limited.